Royal Palm Way, Palm Beach, Florida
MW01628502
"WHITEHALL" THE HOME OF HENRY M. FLAGLER
Ocean Side of New Breakers Hotel, Palm Beach, Florida

Palm Beach...

a Community Tribute

This book is dedicated to all the great Palm Beach photographers who documented this fascinating town, as well as to the memory of my son, Troy Alexander Devine (1980-2013) who was the innovator and art director of this creative work.

This project was completed by the community - for their community.
We pay tribute to them all.

It has been our privilege to be residents of Palm Beach and call many of these individuals and organizations – our friends. I wish to share their incredible history and life stories with you and sincerely hope they will be remembered for many generations to come - as the men and women of Palm Beach who have worked together to build their community and helped change lives for the better.

Olympia and Troy Devine

Palm Beach...

a Community Tribute

Publication Policy: The Publisher, and/or any of its affiliated agents, employees or subcontractors shall not be subject to any liability for: publication omissions, errors, content, failure to circulate or any published/received information from other sources.

Published by:
4 C Business Development Inc. dba Golden Lion Publishing
205 Worth Ave, Suite 201
Palm Beach FL., USA
info@goldenlionpublishing.com

Printed in China
First Printing 2014
ISBN: 978-0-692-34300-5

About the Cover

Our grateful thanks to Biba St Croix and artist, Jonathan Stein for creating the cover concept... a work of art!

PHOTO CREDIT: Brandon Tarpley

"Postcards from Palm Beach - a true paradise!"

Biba St. Croix

Fashionista, Gallerista, Biba St. Croix's signature style is as bold and distinctive as her eye for top quality art. For close to 10 years, Gallery Biba, has served as a prime destination for the work of fine art masters like Picasso, Wesselmann and Magritte to cutting edge works from International emerging talent. Combing the earth for the brightest and most prominent art from Europe, China and here in the United States; Biba seeks out art that is anything but ordinary.

Whether Biba is hosting soirees at her Worth Avenue gallery to help nonprofit organizations or financially nurturing the careers of emerging South Florida artists in need; Biba's devotion to helping others coupled with her flare for all things fine art, designates her as one impressive work of art!!

The experienced buyer and the new collector gain important insights from Ms. St. Croix along with exposure to a stunning array of artists, including Picasso, Flavin, Warhol and emerging artists such as Jonathan Stein.

Biba Gallery, 224A Worth Ave., Palm Beach FL 33480
www.gallerybiba.com

Jonathan Stein

The "King of All Things Bling," Jonathan Stein, is no stranger to dazzling a crowd. His iconic Pop Art hand-cast bronze sculptures are bejeweled with tens of thousands of individually placed Swarovski crystals. A staple artist during Art Basel Miami Beach, Stein's work has been celebrated throughout Europe, Latin America, and having been in countless museums and Art Fairs within New York, Miami, Boston and beyond. Whether working closely with companies like Sanrio on a traveling Hello Kitty museum exhibition, or designing custom works for celebrities like Katy Perry; Jonathan Stein's love of pop culture is contagious.

Stein also serves as the Creative Director for Drops of Hope Inc. a South Florida 501(c)3 non profit that provides free fantasy room makeovers for underprivileged children battling cancer.

Special Acknowledgment - All Chrome Everything Inc.

PHOTO CREDIT: Brandon Tarpley

Acknowledgments

In actuality it was the community of Palm Beach who wrote their own history - and to whom we pay tribute. However, we owe our gratitude to a dedicated team of supporters and professionals who helped fulfill this project's vision. A project started by innovator, Troy Devine (1980-2013) to document the amazing history of the Town of Palm Beach and the philanthropy of its people.

Our team inspired us, journeyed with us. Their support never wavered through the years until completion. Some helped with invaluable editorial facts, others with archival photographic images and some acted as editorial proof readers. Sadly, we lost some of our team along the way as they completed their own life's journey. They are sorely missed and no doubt creating God's work now.

Pages have the associated editorial credits, but we would like to give a special thanks to:

Kathryn Vecellio for having the vision and great sense of community
- as the first supporter to take our project "leap of faith."

All the organizations listed within these pages *(too many to mention here)*
- for their participation and the editorial pages supplied by them.

The following individuals for their creative talent
- writers, proof readers and editors:

Laurel Baker - Project Editor
John Blades - Executive Director, The Flagler Museum *(editorial contributor)*
Jay Boodheshwar - Director of Recreation & Special Projects, The Town of Palm Beach *(historical content)*
The Honorable Mayor Gail L. Coniglio *(brilliant proof reader!)*
Darrell Hofheinz - Palm Beach Daily News *(editorial contributor)*
Kevin Johnson - Senior Conference Manager and
Shari Mantegna - Director of Marketing, The Breakers Hotel *(Breakers editorial)*

The artists for their talented photographic work:

Davidoff Studio - Photography
Lauren Ellis - Graphic Designer
Lucien Capehart - Photography
Jonathan Stein and Biba St. Croix - Cover concept
Mort Kaye and Corby Kaye - Photography
Palm Beach Daily News - Photographic Department
Zachary Seltzer - Graphic Designer

Thank you!
Olympia and Troy Devine

* Although every effort is made by the publishers and editors to include all of those who may need to be thanked, there were so many of the Palm Beach community who graciously gave of their time and support to help this work - it would take another book to document our gratitude to all of them... we thank them all!

Table of Contents

The Town of Palm Beach

The First 100 Years 13

The Architects 47

Historical Places of Interest 65

The Palm Beach Centennial 107

After 100 Years 135

Playing in Paradise 141

The Palm Beach Community

Photographers 155
** Photographers who have documented Palm Beach society and history and so themselves became part of the town's history.*

Community Notables 165
** Palm Beach community notables are recognized for their "tireless efforts to protect and preserve the social, economic and philanthropic endeavors that have distinguished Palm Beach."*
Palm Beach Daily News Centennial publication.

Charities and Organizations 205
** Organizations were invited to participate based on their longevity, town serving participation and great works. These organizations supplied content and images for their editorial pages.*

Project Team 239

The Palm Beach Foundation, Inc. 243

Publication editorial and photographic content credits for *Palm Beach - A Community Tribute* are noted on a per section, or per page, or per image basis where applicable, and as supplied. The Publisher, and/or any of its affiliated agents, employees or subcontractors shall not be subject to any liability for: publication omissions, errors, content, failure to circulate or any published/received information from other sources.

The Town of Palm Beach...

The First 100 Years

The First 100 Years

Editorial: Courtesy of the Town of Palm Beach
and Palm Beach Daily News

Photo: State Archives of Florida, Florida Memory,
http://floridamemory.com/items/show.8481

When the first settlers arrived in what was to become Palm Beach, the entire area was known as "Lake Worth", named for Major General William Jenkins Worth who fought in the Second Seminole War. Pioneers struggled to clear land for their houses and to make room for their crops. The first of the permanent pioneers arrived in 1872. According to early accounts, Palm Beach received its name following the shipwreck of the "Providencia" which washed ashore in January of 1878. Loaded with coconuts bound for Barcelona from Havana, the cargo scattered and was quickly planted by the locals. This first industry introduced coconuts to the states and led to the profusion of palms along the shore. Palm Beach grew from these humble beginnings.

Word of the area's beauty spread northward and by 1880 the first hotel, the Cocoanut Grove House, opened to accommodate tourists whose primary interests were in hunting and fishing. By the early 1890s the island community was well established with several hotels, businesses and winter residents.

The "Providencia" shipwreck off the coast of Palm Beach in 1878.
Photograph of a painting by Eldred Clark Johnson

Key Historical Events and Dates

Photo: State Archives of Florida, Florida Memory, http://floridamemory.com
FM # 160531 Detroit Photographic Co.

1878: The Providencia wrecks off the coast full of 20,000 coconuts – settlers divided up the cargo and planted the seeds of Palm Beach's future glory.

1893: Henry Flagler, Standard Oil tycoon, declares Palm Beach a "veritable paradise".

1894: Flagler's Royal Poinciana Hotel is completed. It was declared the largest wooden structure in the world.

1896: Flagler's FEC Railway arrives in Palm Beach.

1896: Flagler opens the Palm Beach Inn which is later renamed The Breakers in 1901.

1902: Flagler's winter home "Whitehall" is completed.

1907: Telephone service established with 18 phones.

1911: Palm Beach incorporated as a Town.

1911: Original Royal Park Bridge opened.

1925: Palm Beach Town Hall opened.

1929: "The Plan of Palm Beach" is sponsored by the Garden Club of Palm Beach.

1930: Addison Mizner's Memorial Fountain built in Town Square.

1938: Original Flagler Memorial Bridge opened.

1959: Second Royal Park Bridge opened.

1961-1963: President Kennedy's "Winter White House" was referred to as the family's Palm Beach estate.

1971-1977: Earl E.T. Smith, the last United States Ambassador to Cuba, served as Mayor of Palm Beach.

1995: Mar-a-Lago was transformed into the Mar-a-Lago Club.

2005: Royal Park Bridge was reopened with major improvements.

2009: Palm Beach Town Hall restoration completed.

2010: Worth Avenue redesign is completed.

2011: Town of Palm Beach celebrated its Centennial Year.

Displayed is the Breakers Hotel

Courtesy of the Flagler Museum

Henry M. Flagler, Standard Oil tycoon, declared Palm Beach a “veritable paradise ”

Photo: State Archives of Florida, Florida Memory, http://floridamemory.com
FM # PC5291

Henry M. Flagler’s winter home 1902 (forefront) and The Whitehall Hotel on the Eastern shore of Lake Worth

Henry M. Flagler's Hotel Royal Poinciana on Lake Worth

"Carved out of the jungle by pioneer settlers in the 1870s, Palm Beach found itself grandly ushered into Gilded Age opulence in the final decade of the 19th century. That's when Standard Oil tycoon Henry M. Flagler extended his Florida East Coast Railway to Palm Beach, which he envisioned as the crown jewel of his Florida resorts. His mammoth Hotel Royal Poinciana opened on Lake Worth in 1894, followed two years later, on the oceanfront directly opposite, by the Palm Beach Inn, renamed The Breakers in 1901. A year later, Flagler completed his lavish mansion, Whitehall, just south of the Hotel Royal Poinciana, as a wedding present to his third wife, Mary Lily Kenan Flagler."
Courtesy of Palm Beach Daily News

Photo: State Archives of Florida, Florida Memory, http://floridamemory.com
FM # 24568

Aerial view of The Hotel Royal Poinciana

1894

"At its largest, the Hotel Royal Poinciana was bigger than any other wooden hotel on the planet, and its impact on Palm Beach was just as vast. Opened in February 1894 by Standard Oil tycoon and hotel-and–railroad empire builder Henry M. Flagler, the Colonial-style Hotel Royal Poinciana overlooking Lake Worth immediately put Palm Beach on the society map as the de rigueur winter destination of the Gilded Age, offering seasonal guests pastimes ranging from golf and strolls along the lake to tea in its famous Cocoanut Grove. In 1910, a year before Palm Beach was incorporated, more than 2,000 guests attend the annual Washington's Birthday Ball held at the Royal Poinciana Hotel's ballroom The Royal Poinciana would suffer heavy damage in the two hurricanes of the late 1920's. And by the end of 1935, the structure would be demolished."
Courtesy of Palm Beach Daily News

1908

Photo: State Archives of Florida, Florida Memory, http://floridamemory.com
FM # 145901

The Hotel Royal Poinciana Ballroom

Photo: State Archives of Florida, Florida Memory, http://floridamemory.comFM
118116 Series: Louise Frisbie Collection

The Palm Beach Inn renamed The Breakers in 1901

Photo: State Archives of Florida, Florida Memory, http://floridamemory.com
FM # 118329, Series: Louise Frisbie Collection

Pedicabs, or wicker wheel chairs, for the convenience of Flagler Hotel patrons

1887

Photo: State Archives of Florida, Florida Memory, http://floridamemory.comFM # 28167

Horse-drawn railway car passing by The Breakers Hotel

The pioneer era ended in 1894 with the opening of Henry M. Flagler's Royal Poinciana Hotel, followed by the arrival of the Florida East Coast Railroad in 1896. The railroad tracks crossed Lake Worth delivering passengers directly to the Flagler system of hotels: the Hotel Royal Poinciana on the lake and the Palm Beach Inn on the ocean.

Guests made reference to the Palm Beach Inn, referring to it as wanting to be 'down by the breakers'. Flagler changed the name to The Breakers.

Photo: State Archives of Florida, Florida Memory, http://floridamemory.com FM # 10987

Florida East Coast Railway's horse-drawn cart

Man of the Century

by John M. Blades

HENRY FLAGLER

Henry Flagler literally invented modern Florida. And, nowhere is Flagler's legacy more evident than in Palm Beach. At a time in life when the average man of the late 19th century had reached the end of his life expectancy, Henry Flagler decided to step back from the day-to-day responsibilities of Standard Oil, the company he co-founded. Had he not accomplished another thing for the rest of his life, he certainly would be remembered for his role in what would remain for a century the largest and most profitable corporation in the world. But instead of retiring, Flagler devoted all of his considerable resources and creativity to developing Florida.

From St. Augustine to Miami, Henry Flagler built a series of luxury hotels that quickly established tourism as a mainstay of Florida's economy. His Florida East Coast Railway not only connected his hotels but opened the state to growth of all kinds. Southeast. Around 1900, Henry Flagler decided to build a winter home, which he named Whitehall, on the eastern shore of Lake Worth. Whitehall was unlike any of his other homes. It was instead a home for the Muses, a museum and a wedding gift for his wife, **Mary Lily Kenan.**

Built to evoke an image of a temple to Apollo, **Whitehall's** public rooms are filled with symbolism related to the Muses of arts and literature.

In 1960, Whitehall became a public museum and in 2000, a National Historic Landmark.

Around 1900, Henry M. Flagler decided to build a winter home, which he named Whitehall, on the eastern shore of Lake Worth, which was a wedding gift for his wife, Mary Lily Kenan.

Through his Model Land Company, Flagler encouraged the agricultural development of millions of acres, thus establishing agriculture as another mainstay of the state's economy. Not content with those accomplishments, Flagler undertook and accomplished the most ambitious engineering feat ever attempted by a private citizen, the building of the Over-Sea Railroad, covering more than 155 miles from Miami to Key West.

Along the way, Henry Flagler fell in love with the Lake Worth area and decided he would build the Hotel Royal Poinciana on the eastern shore of Lake Worth, where a lush grove of coconut palms had grown up following the shipwreck of the Providencia in 1878 with a cargo of 20,000 coconuts. On the western shore of the Lake, he established a city he named West Palm Beach, which he hoped would one day become a thriving metropolis larger than Jacksonville. The Hotel Royal Poinciana became the world's largest resort, and Greater West Palm Beach indeed grew into a thriving metropolis larger than Jacksonville and the seat of government for one of the largest counties in the

Today, Whitehall is known around the world as one of America's great historic house museums.

Of all the places Henry Flagler established or nurtured, of all the places he could have chosen to live and have his greatest impact, he chose the shores of Lake Worth. Here he gave away thousands of acres for churches, a fire department, a waterworks, a power station, schools, clubs, cemeteries and parks. And, here he built his winter home and Florida's first temple of the arts, the world's largest resort and a thriving metropolis that would become larger than Jacksonville.

While a great many have helped make Palm Beach the beautiful place that it has become over the last century, Palm Beach owes its very existence more to Henry Flagler than to any group of 10 other individuals. No doubt what Henry Flagler would be most proud of is the fact that so many have come to share his love of the place he thought of as "Paradise."

State Archives of Florida, Florida Memory, http://floridamemory.com/items/show/6739

1926

The magnificent stone structure, as it stands today, was completed in 1926. **The Breakers** serves as a Palm Beach landmark and beacon to residents and visitors alike, a reminder of the extraordinary vision Flagler had when he founded the resort in 1896.

While a great many have helped to make the Town of Palm Beach the beautiful and special place that it has become over the last century, Palm Beach owes its distinction and character to Henry Flagler.

Photo: State Archives of Florida, Florida Memory, http://floridamemory.com FM # 160536 Postcard Collection, Publication Credit: E.C. Kropp Co.

1926 - The Palm Beach Hotel was built with a blend of classic Spanish and Mediterranean architecture and modern conveniences - by architect, Mortimer Dickinson Metcalfe. The Palm Beach Hotel was converted to a hotel-codominium in 1990.

Palm Beach Hotel, 235 Sunrise Avenue

Palm Beach Piers

In 1896 Palm Beach was established as a port with The Breakers Pier serving Flagler's Palm Beach to Nassau steamships. Constructed with 1,000 feet of rail tracks, it extended into the Atlantic Ocean. The Breakers Pier allowed passengers to travel to and from Palm Beach - via the Pier's rail cars and the docked traveling vessels. These vessels also brought necessary supplies to Palm Beach.

In 1903 the rail tracks were removed when steamships no longer docked at the pier. It became a recreational fishing spot for many until it was damaged by the hurricane of 1928.

Photo: State Archives of Florida, Florida Memory, http://floridamemory.com
FM # 145858

Frolicking in the surf beside the railroad pier

Photo: State Archives of Florida, Florida Memory, http://floridamemory.com
FM # 160527 Credit: Detroit Photographic Co.

Fishing from the Breakers Pier

Palm Beach Piers
continued

"Although newcomers to Midtown's beach may have a hard time envisioning it, Palm Beach was once famous for its oceanfront piers, including an early one at the Breakers that served guests of that hotel and the Hotel Royal Poinciana; it was damaged in the 1928 hurricane and demolished. In 1925 at the east end of Worth Avenue, Gus Jordahn opened his "Rainbo Pier" – stretching more than 1,000 feet into the ocean and attracting sightseers and anglers – to complement his popular Gus' Baths, two pools connected to the beach by an underground passageway. Jordahn sold the pier in the early 1930's and the new owners renamed it the Palm Beach pier. In the coming decades, the pier's amenities would include a coffee shop, a cocktail lounge, a restaurant with a patio for dancing and easy access to nearby shops. Damaged by hurricanes and other storms, the pier was in such bad shape by 1969 that the town demolished it, although its pilings remained. In 1991, for Palm Beach's 80th birthday, the town installed at its site a brass marker to commemorate the structure. Last year, the plaque was transferred to a new clock tower at the east end of the Avenue – a fitting tribute to Palm Beach's longtime love affair with taking a stroll above the sea."
Courtesy of Palm Beach Daily News

The Clock Tower

At the intersection of Worth Avenue and South Ocean Boulevard

PHOTO CREDIT: Devine

The Clock Tower

2010 - As part of the Worth Avenue re-design, a thirty foot clock tower was built at the entrance of Worth Avenue on South Ocean Boulevard. For a more traditional European look a concrete mix with shells was used for the structure. The tower is a symbolic reminder of the Atlantic Ocean Pier.

The Palm Beach Pier plaque located inside of the clock tower reads, "Erected and opened to the public in 1925, the pier extended out 1095 feet from this point. For over 40 years, it was a favorite town attraction featuring a coffee shop, cocktail, lounge, restaurant, tackle shop and fishermen's lockers. A series of successive storms and hurricanes gradually eroded the structure, causing it to be removed in 1969."

The Garden Club of Palm Beach

Photo: State Archives of Florida, Florida Memory, http://floridamemory.com
FM # 75123, Dept. of Commerce Collection

Royal Palm Way

The Garden Club of Palm Beach, founded in 1928, took on the herculean task of securing a formal town plan, which was accepted by the Town Council in 1930. Since its founding, the organization has brought sound policy positions to the Town of Palm Beach along with a commitment to preserve and protect all that makes Palm Beach unique.

As a member of the Garden Club of America, its members also enjoy the challenges of floral competitions. The club has received numerous national awards over the years for their focus on educational programming and town beautification. Their primary emphasis has been on conservation, civic improvement and horticulture. Their handiwork can be seen on every corner of town.

Initially the club set about with town beautification efforts. Palms were planted along Royal Palm Way, vegetation was added to areas in need of greenery after hurricanes and the Demonstration Garden at the Society of the Four Arts was introduced. Over the years, additional projects were added, including the kaleidoscope plantings on Royal Poinciana Way, the Oasis traffic circle design near the Southern Boulevard Bridge and the extraordinary living wall on Worth Avenue comprised of eleven species as a part of over 10,000 plants.

2013

PHOTO CREDIT: Devine

The Living Wall on Worth Avenue, corner of South County Road

Town Hall

Palm Beach Town Hall, 360 South County Road

Today, the **Palm Beach Town Hall** stands as both a symbol of the history of Palm Beach and as a working municipal building where government meets the challenges of twenty first century life. The Palm Beach Town Hall is a two and a half story Mediterranean Revival style building that was originally designed in 1925 by the architectural firm of Harvey and Clarke as two separate buildings, and joined together by architect John L. Volk in 1967. It is the center piece of an island of outstanding architecture.

When Town Hall was constructed in 1925, it was designed as two individual buildings, both of approximately the same size and scale, and connected by a central open courtyard. The fire station was placed in the two and a half story structure, situated on the north end of the parcel. Municipal offices, the police station, a council chambers that seated three hundred and fifty and a jail were housed in the southern building, which was two stories in height.

On the north end of the building are four large wooden doors of the fire station. To the north of the building, is Addison Mizner's Memorial Fountain, that was constructed in 1929 to honor Palm Beach pioneer families and World War I veterans. To the south of the building, the traffic lanes converge and head toward Worth Avenue, one of the town's main shopping streets. Today, Town Hall is in excellent condition, and although altered over the years to meet the expanding needs of the municipality, it maintains its architectural integrity. Although originally designated as an individual local landmark in 1979, the building is now part of the local Town Hall Square Historic District that was designated by the Landmarks Commission in 1990.

The Palm Beach Town Hall underwent additional restoration in 1989 and 2010. It was added to the National Register of Historic Places on January 28, 2005.

Editorial information from the archives of the Town of Palm Beach Planning, Zoning and Building Department

The First 100 Years
1911 – 1918
"Cap" E.N. Dimick
1918 – 1919
T.T. "Tip" Reese
1930 – 1935
John Shepard, Jr.
1935 – 1953
James M. Owens, Jr.
1979 – 1983
Mack L. Ritchie
1983 – 1993
Yvelyne de Marcellus Marix

1919 – 1922
George W. Jonas

1922 – 1928
Cooper C. Lightbown

1928 – 1930
Barclay H. Warburton

1953 – 1971
Claude D. Reese

1971 – 1977
Earl E.T. Smith

1977 – 1979
William B. Cudahy

1993 – 2000
Paul R. Ilyinsky

2000 - 2005
Lesly S. Smith

2005 – 2011
Jack McDonald

Little Known...

Cocoanut Grove House of Refuge – first hotel in Palm Beach

- The Cocoanut Grove House, once Florida's only hotel on the east coast between Titusville and Key West, stood at this location on Lake Trail. The hotel was originally built in 1876 by Elisha Newton "Cap" Dimick as a private residence for his family. Dimick was one of the co-founders of Palm Beach. He served in the Florida State Legislature from 1890-1903 and as the town's first mayor after its incorporation in 1911. The Cocoanut Grove House opened in 1880 as an inn after Dimick added eight rooms to the building.

- In 1882, Dimick sold the hotel to Commodore Charles Clark. Approximately 4,500 guests visited the hotel between 1883 and 1895, arriving by the Sharpie Illinois, a flat-bottomed boat that sailed between the Indian River and Lake Worth. Hotel guests dined on fish, green turtle, venison, and vegetables for $1.50 a day by the week or $6 a day. In 1893, Henry M. Flagler, who had decided to extend the Florida East Coast Railroad to Palm Beach, stayed at the Cocoanut Grove House. While visiting there he envisioned his famous Royal Poinciana Hotel. Flagler later rented the hotel for his workers while they were building the Royal Poinciana. In October 1893, the Cocoanut Grove House was destroyed by fire. *Source: The Florida Historical Marker on Lake Trail*

- Elisha "Cap" Dimick was known as a man of firsts. He was the first Palm Beach mayor, opened the first bank and in 1880 opened the first Palm Beach hotel, the Cocoanut Grove House. His statue now stands on the southwestern top of the Royal Poinciana Way median.

- Millie and Jacob Gildersleeve, two of the earliest African-American pioneers on the island, purchased property from Elisha Dimick in 1890, which later became Riviera Beach.

"Cap" E.N. Dimick

- The Town of Palm Beach, Palm Beach County's second municipality, was incorporated on April 17, 1911. Town fathers hastened the incorporation upon hearing that West Palm Beach was planning to annex the island resort during the 1911 legislative session. Thirty-five men met at the Palm Beach Hotel and voted to incorporate.

- They elected the first town officials: Elisha N. Dimick, Mayor; John P. McKenna, Town Clerk; Joseph Borman, Marshal and J. B. Donnelly, William Fremd, John W. Doe, Enoch Root, and J. J. Ryman, councilmen. It was not until 1929, however, that preparation of a Town Plan was sponsored by the Garden Club of Palm Beach.

Photo: State Archives of Florida, Florida Memory, http://floridamemory.com/items/show/44115
FM # 40092

The Breakers Hotel on Fire

- The Breakers Hotel burned down twice, first in 1903 and then again in 1925. The 1925 fire lead to embers falling on The Palm Beach Hotel across the island... and that wood-framed hotel also burned to the ground.

Early 1900, Alligator Joe's Pavilion on Worth Avenue

- In the early 1900s Alligator Joe was an early businessman on Worth Avenue. At the western end of the avenue, Joe ran Alligator Joe's Farm, where he entertained winter visitors by holding wrestling matches with his alligators. He charged twenty-five cents to see his wrestling show and an additional twenty-five cents to walk the trail of tropical vegetation and wildlife. Alligator Joe's trail later became Worth Avenue.

- Wicker pedicabs were the main mode of travel in Palm Beach where automobiles did not have access. They took Palm Beach guests from their rail cars, as well as from steamships arriving at the piers en route to Palm Beach hotels and on sight-seeing tours of the resort island.

State Archives of Florida, Florida Memory
http://floridamemory.com/items/show/12212

Henry M. Flagler being driven in pedicab

Photo: State Archives of Florida, Florida Memory
http://floridamemory.com
PC # 7272

Wicker pedicabs on Lake Trail

"In 1890 Laura Woodward focused much of her painting on the coconut palms of Palm Beach and also portrayed the resplendent Royal Poinciana tree blossoms and other flora that bloomed in the late spring and the summer months. She showed these lush renderings in St. Augustine and soon Henry Flagler focused rapt attention upon them. He was not only impressed with the paintings but also her tales of this tropical paradise. Her cousin later recalled that Laura "told all who would listen of the beauties of Palm Beach and its potentialities. Flagler was one who listened."

Laura Woodward: "The Artist Behind the Innovator Who Developed Palm Beach," by Deborah C. Pollack.

The Architects

Architecture – as art and history – is a significant feature of Palm Beach. As the town evolved from a destination to one that included private residences, the most talented architects of the day found thier way to Palm Beach and left an indelible mark on the town's image and its history. **Laurel Baker**

Photo: State Archives of Florida, Florida Memory, http://floridamemory.com
FM # 165177

1920s

The Architects

Architecture – as art and history – is a significant contributor to Palm Beach. With the town's evolution from a hotel-tourist destination to one of private residents, the most talented architects of the day found the way to Palm Beach and left an indelible mark on the town's image and its history. These early architects formed the Art Jury for Palm Beach, a committee created to ensure the quality of buildings befitting the town. This early attention to development and growth led to the formation of the Architectural Review Commission, aptly seated in Town Hall, a building with a long and honorable history.

The earliest buildings were made from locally available materials – wood and palm fronds when the earliest tourists came for hunting and fishing. The railroad brought another wave of visitors, these staying for longer periods in growing hotels, again made of wood but enormous in scale. Palm Beach became the leading American resort. As will be seen, the early architects often worked together on projects, bringing their unique signature styles to a grand finale.

Worth Avenue

Addison Mizner

Addison Mizner 1872-1933

Photo: State Archives of Florida, Florida Memory, http://floridamemory.com FM # 1459

With the arrival of Paris Singer and Addison Mizner in late 1916, the money and the imagination team, a whole new era of style and practicality and excess descended upon Palm Beach. Singer (23rd child of Isaac Singer, founder of the Singer Manufacturing Company), wanted to build a hospital for the returning wounded of World War I and had his globe-trotting friend, Mizner, design a building at the western edge of Worth Avenue. Flamboyant, decadent, excessive – let it tell a story grander than the next: this was Mizner's motto.

Mizner's entrepreneurial spirit led him to build the industries needed to provide the materials for these pleasure palaces: colorful tiles, wrought iron, barrel tiles, pots and accessories, even the furniture. He worked on 38 projects in Palm Beach, earning him the title of 'father of Palm Beach architecture.' The Mediterranean Revival style has been replicated; his idea taken from historic towns in Europe - the buildings were organic, changing over time to reflect different needs and uses.

The Everglades Club, Worth Avenue

1919 - As World War I ended the hospital became a private club. The Everglades Club began with twenty-five charter members, with Paris Singer as the President.

1920 - The Club had additions of a nine-hole golf course, eleven apartments and sixteen shops.

1918 - The Everglades Club on Worth Avenue: Paris Singer (23rd child of Isaac Singer, founder of the Singer Manufacturing company) together with his friend, the architect Addison Mizner, decided that they would build a hospital. During World War I only war-related buildings could be built. Singer had previously built three hospitals in France.

Maisonette and tennis courts at the Everglades Club

Addison Mizner

2013
PHOTO CREDIT: Devine

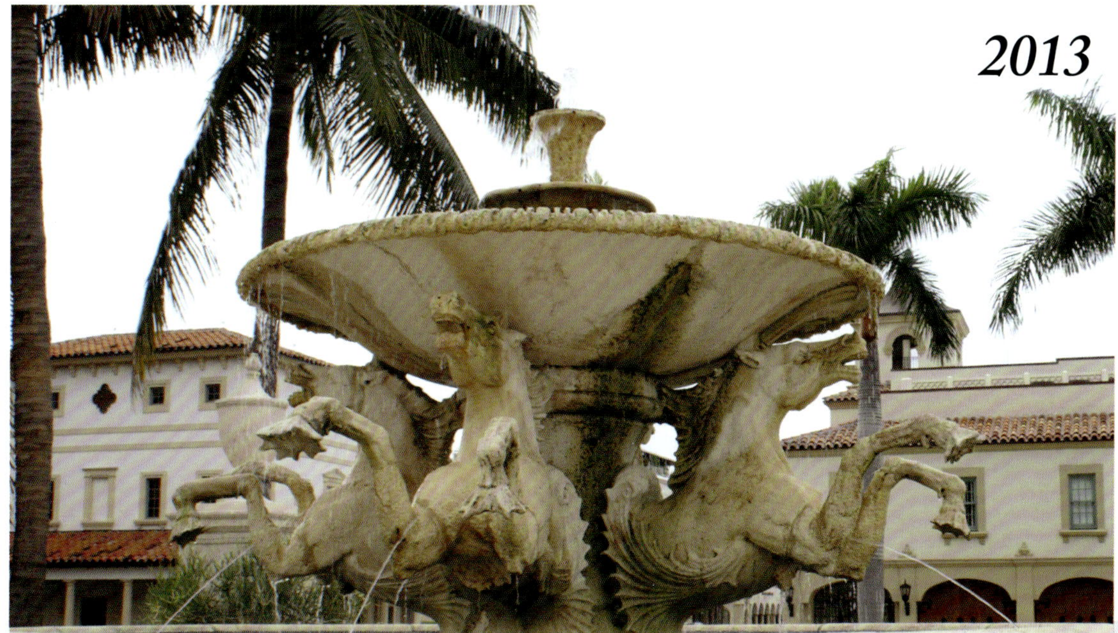

The Memorial Fountain, in the commercial heart of town

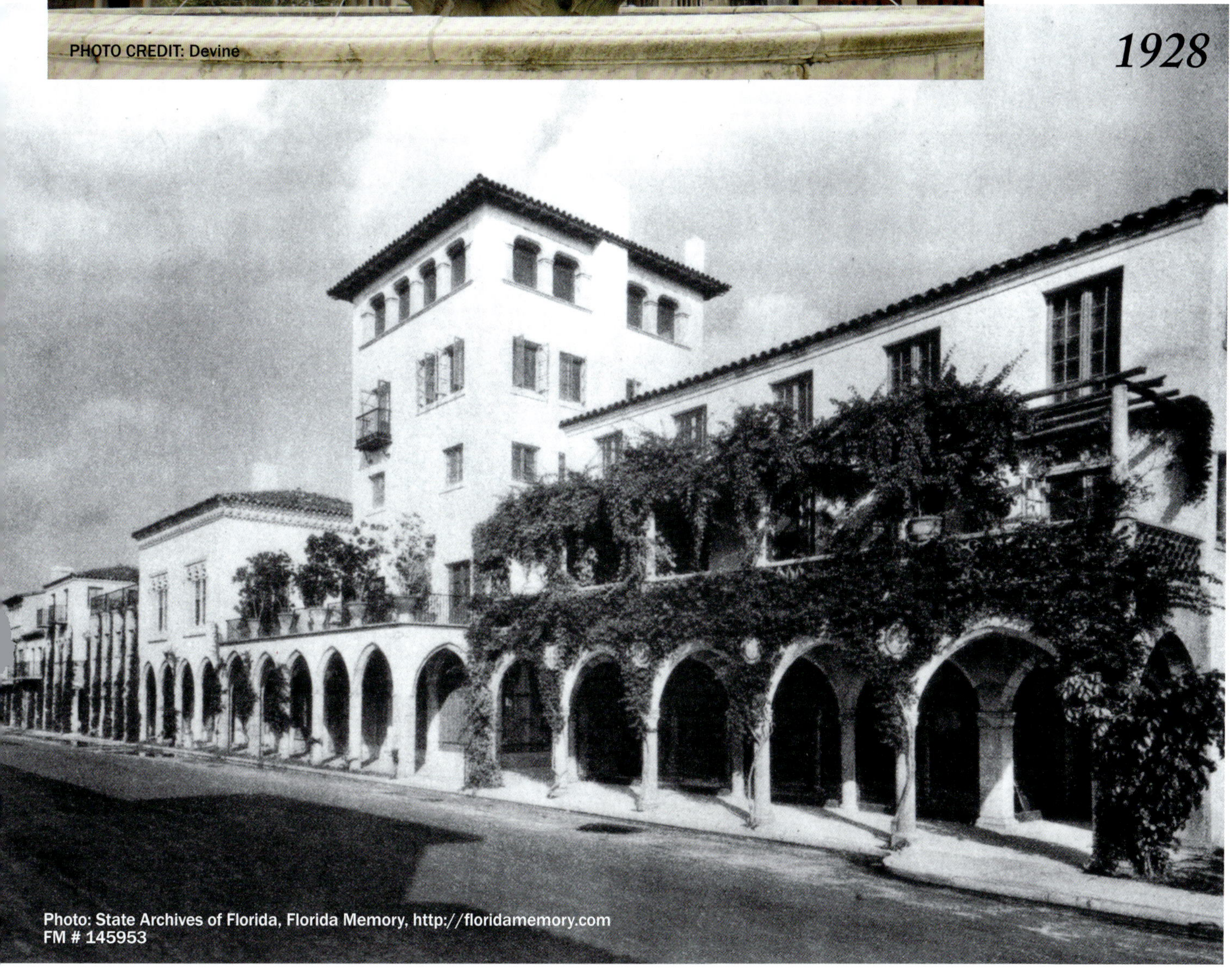
1928
Photo: State Archives of Florida, Florida Memory, http://floridamemory.com
FM # 145953

Worth Avenue Shopping Arcade, constructed in 1924

Joseph Urban

Does art imitate life or visa versa? Theatrical designer and architect Joseph Urban loved the dramatic – stage sets set the mood for over-the-top performances in private homes. These dramatic creations exuded luxury and exoticism. While Urban worked with Wyeth, who brought the more subdued elements to the designs, together their creation of Mar-a-Lago blended the entire stage craft – every sense was tantalized by design from the smell of the ocean, the touch of the breeze, the visual delights of murals and sparkling chandeliers, the haunting musical rhythm of the ocean and the wind surrounding the entire setting with a delicious sense of exotic flavors.

Photo: State Archives of Florida, Florida Memory, http://floridamemory.com
FM # 6746

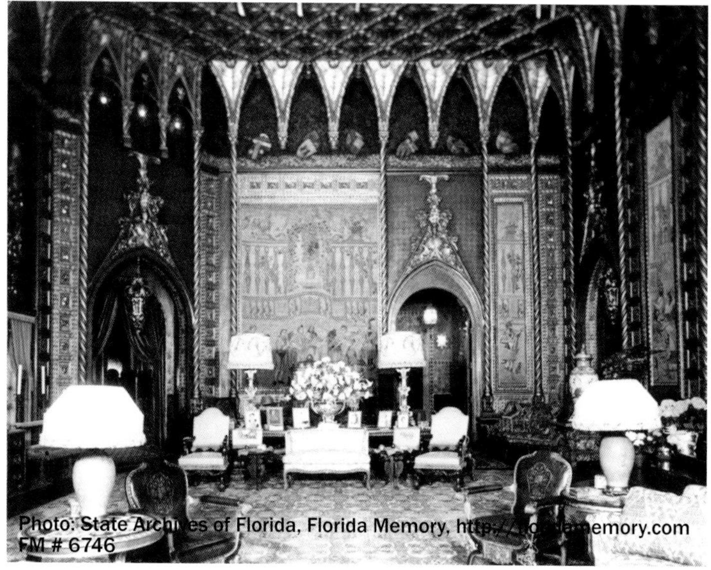

Living Room of The Mar-a-Lago Club

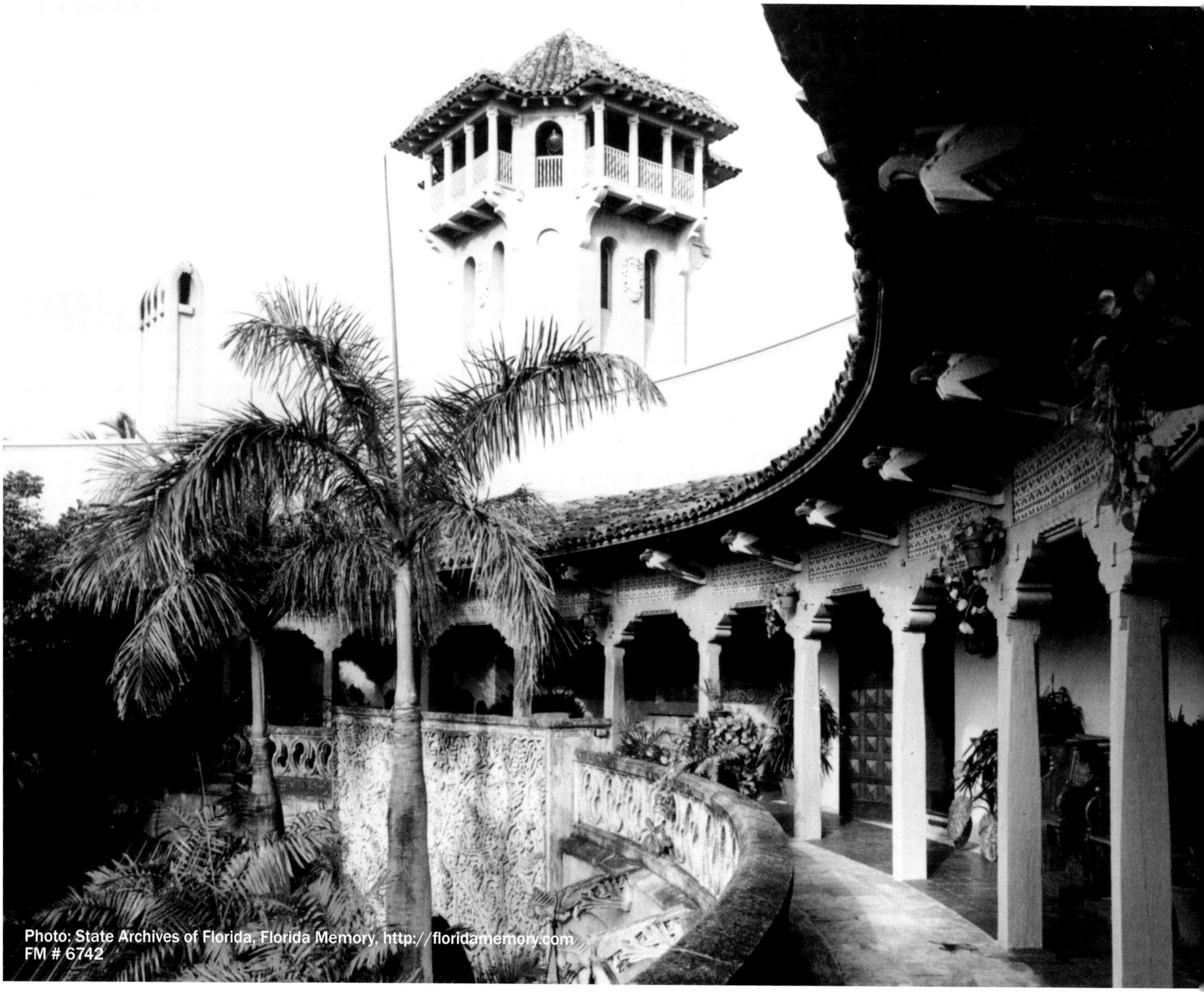
Photo: State Archives of Florida, Florida Memory, http://floridamemory.com
FM # 6742

Upstairs arches of The Mar-a-Lago Club

Joseph Urban

Other notable buildings under Urban's directions included the Paramount Theatre and the Bath and Tennis Club.

Photo: State Archives of Florida, Florida Memory, http://floridamemory.com
FM # 118400 Louise Frisbie Collection

The Paramount Theatre, North County Road

PHOTO CREDIT: Bob Davidoff

The Bath and Tennis Club, South Ocean Boulevard

Howard Major

Major saw Palm Beach differently – adapting his designs to the natural surroundings and eliminating the drama in favor of understated elegance. While favoring Greek Revival architecture, he felt that the Bermuda and West Indies styles were more appropriate and allowed houses to take advantage of the natural breezes. Houses blended more completely into the environment. Form and function were joined allowing for comfort and style. Two signature features to his works include capped chimneys and octagonal windows.

The enduring qualities of his design responded favorably to changing economies while taking full advantage of the abounding natural beauty of the area. Major created homes in Palm Beach, as well as six Bermuda-style houses with zero lot lines on Peruvian Avenue, known as *Major Alley*.

PHOTO CREDIT: Devine

Major Alley, Peruvian Avenue

PHOTO CREDIT: Devine

Marion Sims Wyeth

Wyeth used many of Mizner's elements in the building of his houses but applied his classical training to the designs, with an emphasis on making the outside an integral part of the entire house.

There is a quiet beauty to his work that "speaks through" various architectural styles. Such design allowed for the adaptive restoration of one house into condominium units without compromising the original structure.

Notable amongst his works is Mar-a-Lago, done in collaboration with Joseph Urban.

PHOTO CREDIT: Devine

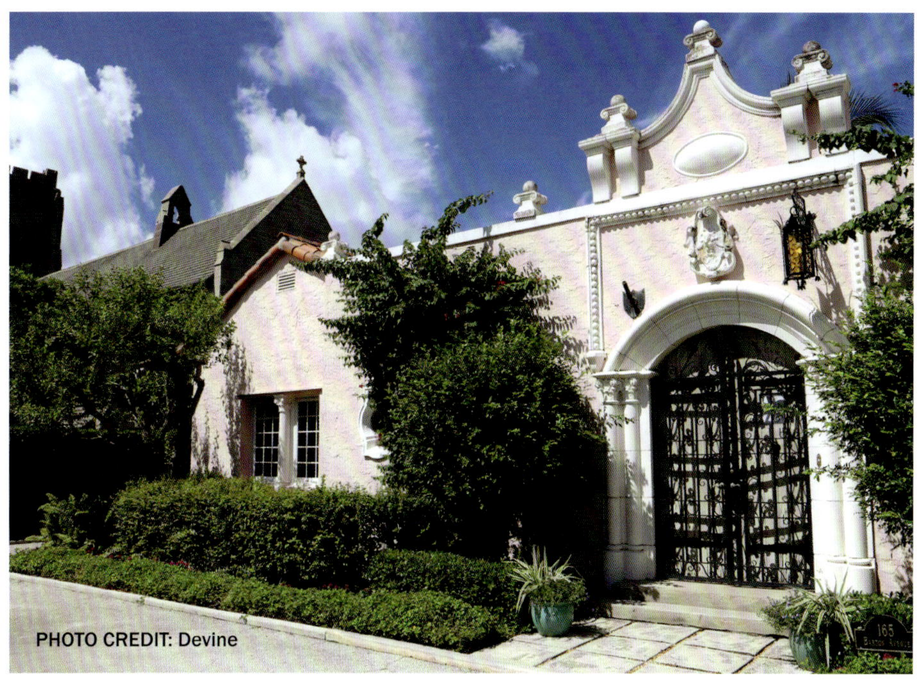

Episcopal Church of Bethesda-by-the-Sea Rectory

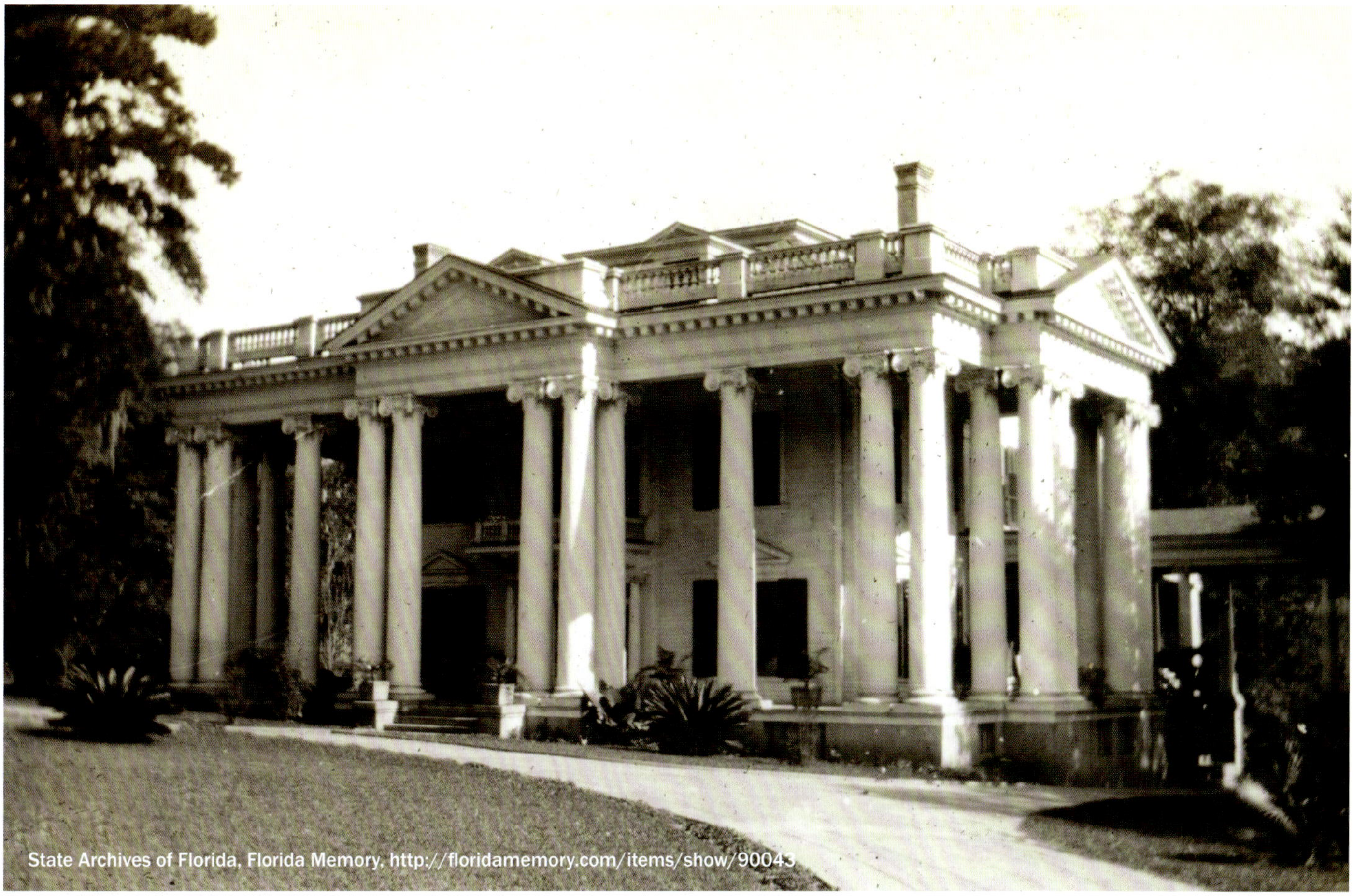
State Archives of Florida, Florida Memory, http://floridamemory.com/items/show/90043

The Florida Governor's Mansion

Maurice Fatio

In his long career, Maurice Fatio's work as a master architect included a full range of styles, including Art Deco. Locally, one can appreciate the magnitude of his work by visiting the First National Bank building, the courtyard in Via Amoré and The Society of the Four Arts Library.

Perhaps the most genteel and urbane of the early architects, Fatio's work displayed more of an Italian influence. His story for a house was to relate a more sensitive, operatic, romantic historic journey over time.

The First National Bank drive-thru banking

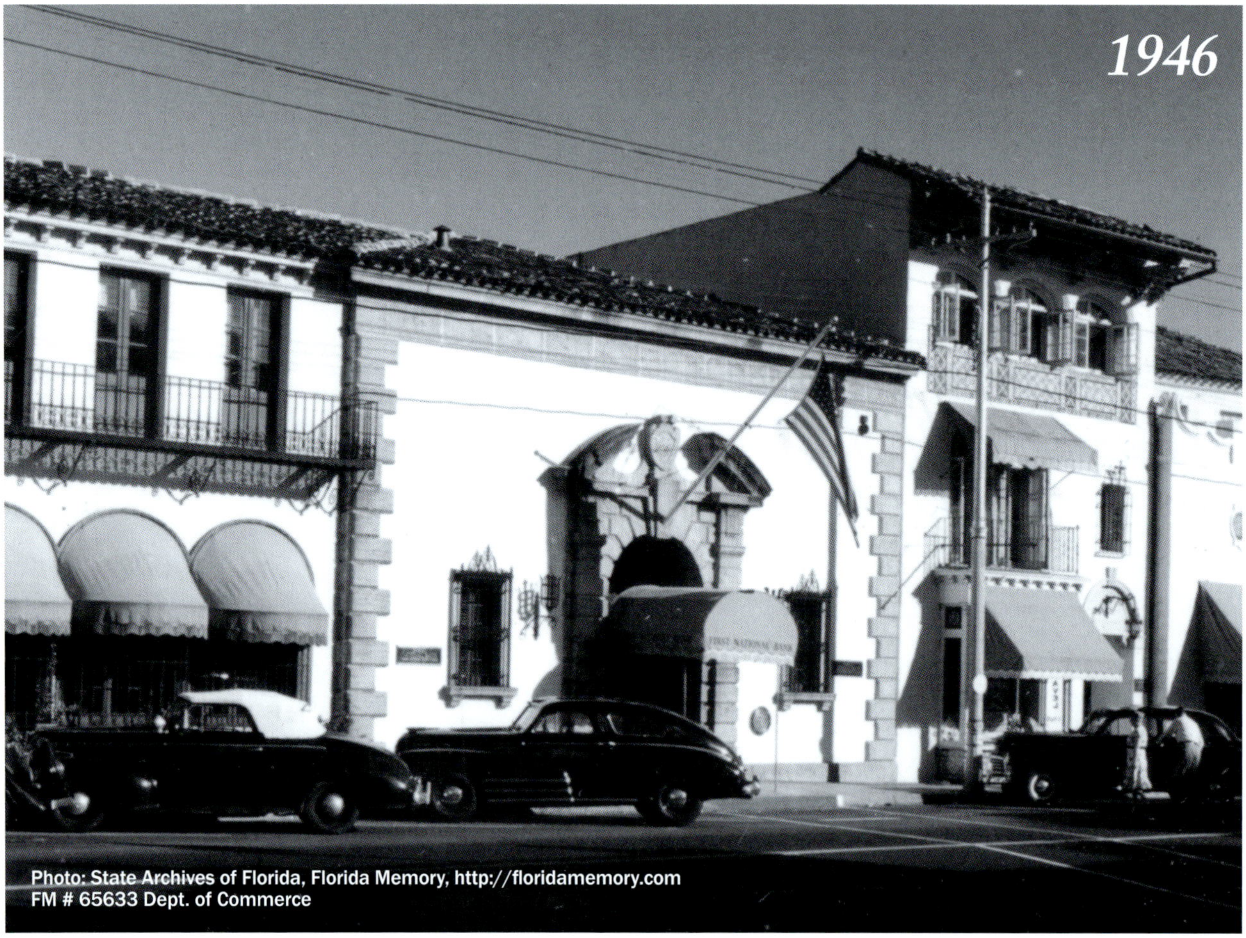

1946

Photo: State Archives of Florida, Florida Memory, http://floridamemory.com
FM # 65633 Dept. of Commerce

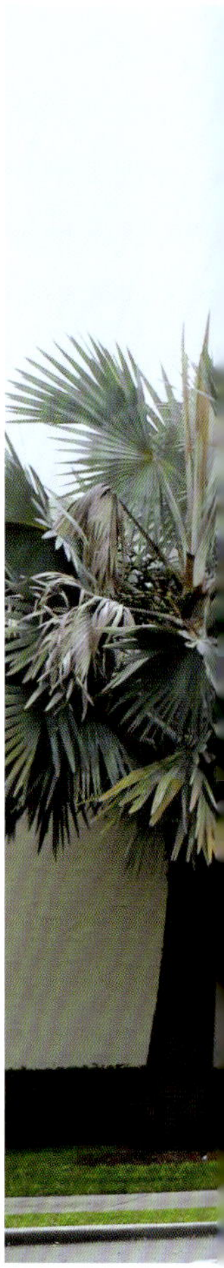

The First National Bank building, South County Road (Wells Fargo Bank)

Maurice Fatio

PHOTO CREDIT: Devine

Via Amoré on Worth Avenue

The Society of the Four Arts Library, Four Arts Plaza

John Volk

Bringing his classical European training to Palm Beach, Volk enjoyed a prolific career which began in 1925. The cool elegance of his works reflects an adaption to changing social and cultural conditions. Volk is credited with the careful blending of Neo-classical British Colonial style with the unique characteristic of South Florida. Houses abound on the island, as do commercial undertakings, notably the Poinciana Plaza and the Poinciana Theatre on Royal Poinciana Way. His contributions to the architectural history of Palm Beach are legendary.

PHOTO CREDIT: Bob Davidoff

John and Jane Volk

PHOTO CREDIT: Bob Davidoff

Party reception at the Trosby Gallery at the Royal Poinciana Plaza

Poinciana Plaza
A Legacy of Notable Shoppers

Poinciana Plaza, Royal Poinciana Way

PHOTO CREDIT: Bob Davidoff

Bing Crosby, Mrs. Peterson and Chris Dunphy

PHOTO CREDIT: Bob Davidoff

Mark and Mary Alice Firestone out strolling

The Celebrity Room at the Royal Poinciana Playhouse staged many a fine production for the era and hosted numerous glamorous cast parties, with many a celebrity guest giving an impromptu performance. Palm Beachers rubbed shoulders with celebrities and royals – all dancing the night away. Among the visitors: Carol Channing, Rita Merano, the Duke and Duchess of Windsor, Elizabeth Taylor, Lauren Becall, Bob Hope, Andy Williams, Bing Crosby, Zsa Zsa Gabor, Burt Reynolds, Kenny Miller, Christopher Plummer and others. The Celebrity Room later became The Poinciana Club. The Royal Poinciana Playhouse was closed in 2004.

PHOTO CREDIT: Bob Davidoff

The Celebrity Room at the Royal Poinciana Playhouse

Celebrity Room Guests

PHOTO CREDIT: Bob Davidoff

Marjorie Merriweather Post with the Duke of Windsor

PHOTO CREDIT: Bob Davidoff

Rosemary Clooney performing at the John F. Kennedy Memorial Hospital Ball

PHOTO CREDIT: Bob Davidoff

The Duke and Duchess of Windsor

PHOTO CREDIT: Bob Davidoff

Earl Blackwell, Kathy Crosby, Frank Hale and Zsa Zsa Gabor

PHOTO CREDIT: Bob Davidoff

Tennis great, Frank Parker and James H. Kimberly

Little Known...

Carrère and Hastings and Horace Trumbauer

by John Blades

Surprisingly two of America's most influential architectural firms are often overlooked when discussing the architects who worked in Palm Beach. First and foremost is of course the firm of Carrère and Hastings. Almost immediately after leaving McKim, Mead, and White to form their own firm in 1886, Carrère and Hastings were fortunate enough to acquire their first major client and commission when Henry Flagler chose them to design his first hotel in St. Augustine, the Hotel Ponce de Leon. They not only designed the Ponce de Leon, they designed another hotel and two churches commissioned by Flagler.

By the time Henry Flagler decided to build a home in Palm Beach, about fifteen years later in 1902, Carrère and Hastings had become so prominent on the national scene among the many projects they were working on at the time were the New York Public Library and the Pan-American. The firm of Carrère and Hastings was in fact so well regarded, not just nationally but internationally, that it was one of only four American firms to be awarded a gold medal by the Royal Institute of British Architects.

The equally well regarded architectural firm of Horace Trumbauer was slated to follow suite in Palm Beach designing a Beaux-Arts mansion like Whitehall for Edward and Eva Stotesbury, much as he had done when he designed many homes outside Philadelphia, like Whitemarsh Hall for the Stotesburys and Lynnewood Hall for the Wideners, the Philadelphia Museum of Art, and the Elms in Newport. Surprisingly, though Eva Stotesbury apparently initially also chose Trumbauer to design their Palm Beach home, she changed her mind and chose instead a young architect just getting started in Palm Beach, Addison Mizner. However, while the estate Mizner designed for the Stoteburys no longer exists, Trumbauer did end up designing an important building here in the Palm Beach area in the late 1920s that still stands today, a Greek Revival temple commissioned for the First Church of Christ, Scientist, on the west end of the Royal Park bridge.

Mortimer Dickerson Metcalfe

by John Blades

Who was Mortimer Dickerson Metcalfe you may ask? Take a walk up Sunrise Avenue and as you admire the Mediterranean Revival style of The Palm Beach Hotel and the beauty of St. Edward's Church you may begin to appreciate Metcalfe's design skills. If that isn't enough, stroll by the old Palm Beach Post Office at the bottom of Royal Poinciana Way, or the next time you're in New York you can admire his work as one of the architects who designed the Grand Central Terminal.

PHOTO CREDIT: Devine

"Educated at the École des Beaux-Arts, architects John Carrère and Thomas Hastings employed location, building orientation, and symbolism in the design of Whitehall and its grounds in order to evoke the sense of a temple to Apollo. As homes for Apollo's Muses of literature and the arts, temples to Apollo were the world's first museums (the word museum literally means home of the Muses) and in the strictest sense of the word Whitehall was Florida's first museum..." *Courtesy of: www.flaglermuseum.us*

Historical Places of Interest

Footsteps through the halls of history echo glorious memories of a hundred years... follow the path, listen to the voices and appreciate the gracious beauty of the Palm Beach spirit. **Troy Devine**

Historial Places of Interest

PHOTO CREDIT: Devine

The Memorial Fountain is situated on the upper terrace of Memorial Park on South County Road. Designed by architect Addison Mizner as one of his final projects. The inspiration for the fountain was the Sea Horses, an 18th-century work by Christopher Unterberger in Rome's Villa Borghese .

The Memorial Fountain Park was dedicated in 1925 in memory of Henry M. Flagler and Elisha N. Dimick.

The Memorial fountain was presented to the Town of Palm Beach as a gift from its residents.

A World War II memorial plaque was added to the park in 1985 to recognize Palm Beach veterans.

The Breakers Palm Beach

When Henry Morrison Flagler, founder of The Breakers, first visited Florida from the northern US in 1878, he had already accumulated a vast fortune as a longtime partner of John D. Rockefeller in the Standard Oil Company. In 1883, he turned his entrepreneurial vision south to Florida, instigated by concern for his ailing wife's health. Impressed with its mild winter climate, he began paving the way for development and tourism with his Florida East Coast Railroad and construction of resort hotels along the coast.

In 1893, Flagler extended the Railroad to isolated Lake Worth, developed the town now known as West Palm Beach on 200 acres along Lake Worth's west shore, and constructed the Royal Poinciana Hotel on its east shore, which became Palm Beach. With easy access via rail, America's most socially prominent families crowded into the tiny island town of Palm Beach to stay at his six-story, Georgian-style Royal Poinciana Hotel. Due to demand, Flagler built a second hotel - the Palm Beach Inn - on the beachfront portion of the Royal Poinciana's property

overlooking the Atlantic Ocean. The Inn opened in January 1896, fully booked for most of that winter season. Many regular Palm Beach guests asked for oceanfront rooms "down by the breakers;" when Flagler doubled the size of the Palm Beach Inn for the 1901 season, accordingly he renamed it The Breakers. A year later, he enlisted Alexander H. Findlay, father of American golf, to design Florida's first golf course adjacent to the Palm Beach Inn.

In 1903, as workers enlarged the wood building for the fourth time in less than a decade, The Breakers burned down. Just two weeks after the fire, Flagler, 73, announced The Breakers would be rebuilt for the upcoming winter season. The Breakers re-opened in 1904 to universal acclaim with 425 rooms, a "who's who" guest register of early-20th century America: Rockefellers, Vanderbilts, and Astors; tycoons Andrew Carnegie and J.P. Morgan; publisher William Randolph Hearst; assorted European nobility and U.S. presidents.

In 1925, 12 years after Henry Flagler's death, tragedy again struck his empire with another fire, accidentally caused by a guest's electrical appliance; fortunately no lives were lost. Flagler's heirs re-built the current Breakers in a record-breaking 11½ months at a cost of $7 million to open just after Christmas 1926 and in time for the start of the Palm Beach season. Its magnificent Italian Renaissance exterior design is complemented by interior décor featuring spectacular Venetian chandeliers, Renaissance paintings, gold-leaf and hand-painted Florentine ceilings, and spectacular 16th - 18th-century tapestries.

In 1942, The Breakers became the U.S. Army's Ream General Hospital, where thousands of servicemen and women recuperated during World War II, drawing prominent visitors such as Eleanor Roosevelt and President Harry Truman. From 1942-44, more than a dozen "Breakers Babies" were born at the hotel.

The Breakers Palm Beach continues Henry Flagler's legacy of excellence, thriving today in the hands of his descendants, the Kenan family (through Flagler's third wife, Mary Lily Kenan), who own and operate the hotel as an entity of Flagler System, Inc. Thanks to their relentless dedication to The Breakers for the long-term, they have committed $25 million to be re-invested in property enhancements each year. This extraordinary capital infusion represents a continuous balance of preservation and modernization; to safeguard and revitalize the resort's historic elements, while seamlessly integrating new amenities to bolster its contemporary appeal for generations to come. Equally noteworthy, The Breakers is the longest continuously operating business in the state of Florida. *Courtesy of The Breakers Hotel*

Now into its second century, The Breakers Palm Beach continues Henry Flagler's legacy of excellence...

In 1889, with courage and vision, the founding members of Bethesda built a one-room sanctuary out of driftwood and packing crates and became the only Episcopal parish in southeast Florida. Bethesda parishioners also created much of the social fabric of what would become Palm Beach, organizing and leading social service and cultural activities in addition to religious services for the entire community.

In 1894, a second, larger church building was completed. It still stands on North Lake Way and today is a private residence. Several decades later, in 1925, a larger nave befitting of the beauty and grandeur of the island rose up in the heart of town. The historical chronicle note that "The Church of Bethesda-by-the-Sea had... been in the center of all that was finest in spirit in the community for thirty-six years." And so it remains today—125 years later.

Bethesda-by-the-Sea

141 South County Road, Palm Beach, FL 33480
www.bbts.org

Bethesda is a vibrant and joyful Episcopal community of people from all walks of life, whose mission and joy is to experience the clear and strong presence of God and to understand and spread Christ's teachings through collective worship, learning, and service. This is a sanctuary, a place of rest from hurried lives. Everyone who stops by feels the peaceful presence of God in this place.

The Royal Poinciana Chapel

60 Cocoanut Row, Palm Beach, FL

"The Royal Poinciana Chapel began in 1897 by one man with a clear-cut and determined hope. In 2009 over a century later the Chapel remains strong because of the many glad participants of this engaging, caring community of faith who love God, enjoy the Chapel and who participate into its mission.Generosity and vision transformed a wilderness into the paradise that is The Royal Poinciana Chapel today..." www.royalpoincianachapel.org

PHOTO CREDIT: Devine

The Olivia Kiebach Gardens

PHOTO CREDIT: Devine

St. Edward, 144 North County Road
Palm Beach, FL 33480

In the early 1920s, the national economy was such that an increasing number of Americans - rich and not so rich - were finding more time and money to spend on vacations away from home.

Travel was in their blood. Prior to those years, only the very wealthy could afford a trip to the warm South in the winter months and Palm Beach was their first choice. Gradually, however, the number of travelers to this area increased to the point where hotel building could hardly keep up with the demand for temporary accommodations.

It was at such a time that the need was felt for a Catholic Church to serve the needs of the hundreds of visitors and permanent residents who had to travel miles to hear Mass on Sundays and had no facility for religious celebrations. About this time, a visionary Jesuit priest, Father Felix Clarkson, sought and was given permission by the Most Rev. Patrick Barry, Bishop of St. Augustine, to purchase three lots at the corner of North County Road and Sunrise Avenue for the purpose of establishing a "mission" church.

http://www.stedwardpb.com

PHOTO CREDIT: Devine

St. Edward Church

Ground was broken for the future church on April 4, 1926, Easter Sunday. A small band of the faithful were led by the Rev. Felix J. Clarkson, S.J., to witness the ground-breaking on a plot that was to become St. Edward Church. According to our records there were about twenty people who heard Father Clarkson bless the ground and observe Colonel Edward R. Bradley turn over the first spadeful of dirt. So, without fanfare, a few curious onlookers and passersby witnessed that a great work was begun. Little did they know that they were seeing the planting of an acorn that grew into the mighty oak that is St. Edwards today.

Little Red Schoolhouse — first school in Southeast Florida

Founded in 1886 as a community project, the Little Red Schoolhouse was the first one-room school built in southeastern Florida. With $200 for lumber from the Dade County School Board, the men of the community, led by George W. Lainhairt volunteered their labor to construct the 22-by-40- foot building. The school's original location was one mile north of the Flagler Memorial Bridge on Lake Trail on land donated by the David Brown and John C. Hoagland families. The Ladies Aid Society raised additional money for the school's furnishings. Sixteen- year- old Hattie Gale taught the first class of eight students ranging in age from six to seventeen. Pupils arrived by boat, bicycle, or on foot. The school served families around Lake Worth until 1901. It was then turned into a gardener's shed on the John S. Phipps property. In 1960 the structure was moved to Phipps Ocean Park and renovated by the Gardeners Society of Palm Beach. The Preservation Foundation of Palm Beach restored the building to its historic appearance in 1990 and leases it for the foundation's pioneer education program.

Source: Florida Heritage Site Marker

PHOTO CREDIT: Devine

Palm Beach Day Academy

Two Schools Share a Birthday

"Palm Beach Day Academy and Palm Beach Public School share an anniversary in common; Both opened in 1921. The original Palm Beach School for Boys and the Palm Beach School for Girls later merged to become Palm Beach Private School, which, in time, became Palm Beach Day School. It is today called Palm Beach Day Academy, having merged in 2006 with the Academy of the Palm Beaches. At first open only seasonally, today the school serves pre-kindergarten through ninth-graders with a traditional school term at its longtime home on Seaview Avenue. Palm Beach Public School, meanwhile, began as a two-room school building on the southeast corner of Cocoanut Row and Seaview Avenue, was expanded in 1923, and in 1927 became the only combined elementary-middle school in Palm Beach County – a status it held until the mid-1990s. A new west building, later enlarged, transformed the campus in 1929; in 2006, the student body of elementary-age students moved into their new building that replaced the outdated one on the east side of Cocoanut Row. Generations of students – private Bulldogs and public Comets – have passed through the doors of both institutions. And although the vast majority of those who attend Palm Beach Public do not live on the island, the alumni of both institutions can proudly say: "I went to school in Palm Beach."
Courtesy of Palm Beach Daily News

PHOTO CREDIT: Devine

Palm Beach Public School

When it was completed in 1902, the New York Herald proclaimed that Whitehall, Henry Flagler's home in Palm Beach, was "more wonderful than any palace in Europe, grander and more magnificent than any other private dwelling in the world." As wonderful as Whitehall was in 1902, and remains today, it was built to be, and has always been, so much more than a house.

Whitehall, the house museum that Henry Flagler built, may be one of the purest expressions of the Gilded Age trend of building monumental communication devices, and the message is most clear where Carrère and Hastings concentrated the greatest amount of effort, in the facade and the Grand Hall. For Whitehall's facade, Carrère and Hastings designed an entrance framed by massive columns that looks very much like a temple to Apollo, where the Muses would reside.

Built in just 18 months, Whitehall was intended to be both a monumental example of high culture and high technology. In 1900, when construction began, Palm Beach was one of the least developed and most remote locations in the United States.

PHOTO CREDIT: Devine

Whitehall

It was arguably America's last frontier. However, with 22 bathrooms, electric lighting, central heating, and a telephone system, Whitehall was not only an impressive statement of high culture, but perhaps the most technologically advanced home in America. As huge crews worked around the clock to complete Whitehall in such a short time, Flagler wrote to the furniture and decorating firm of Pottier and Stymus saying, "I too wonder how you have accomplished so much in such a short time... but I trust that when it is finished, you will have the satisfaction of contemplating it as the greatest job of your life."

Today, Whitehall is a National Historic Landmark and a public house museum that has been visited by millions from around the world. It stands as a monument to a time when the American character we celebrate was born from a unique series of events that came together in history only one time and in only one place - here, in America. Florida could not have hoped for a more appropriate or impressive place as its first museum ."

John Blades, Executive Director

www.flaglermuseum.us

PHOTO CREDIT: Devine

If these walls could talk...

In 1926, the **Paramount Theatre Building** was designed by Joseph Urban in the Moorish Revival and Spanish Colonial Revival styles. It is a historic movie palace and theater located at 139 North County Road and Sunrise Avenue, Palm Beach, Florida. The Paramount hosted movies, charitable events, concerts and even bond appeals during World War II.

From 1927 to 1980 many world-renowned performers graced the Paramount stage and screen. The passageway walls are covered with historical photographs as an exhibit. This exhibit includes thousands of notable guests, royalty and presidents who came to enjoy and pay homage to the artists. In 1973, it was added to the U.S. National Register of Historic Places.

The Paramount Theatre Building now houses the Paramount Church, a non-denominational Christian church. The Senior Pastor and Founder of Paramount Church is Rev. Dwight Stevens.

www.paramountchurchpb.com

Constructed in 1886 by R.R. McCormick, a Denver railroad developer, **Sea Gull Cottage** was purchased by Henry Flagler in 1893 and became Flagler's first winter residence in Palm Beach. In 1894 Sea Gull was moved and restored by the Preservation Foundation of Palm Beach. It is now the Parish House of the Royal Poinciana Chapel.
Florida Historical Marker

Sea Gull Cottage – Oldest House
60 Coconut Row

Palm Beach Daily News Building
318 Brazillian Avenue

"In 1913 **The Palm Beach Daily News** moves into a building on Brazilian Avenue, which becomes known as the Palm Beach Daily News Building. The Palm Beach Daily News was founded in 1897 as the Daily Lake Worth News. The Weekly Palm Beach Life Magazine, established in 1906, is the newspaper's sibling publication."
Courtesy of Palm Beach Daily News

The **William Gray Warden House** was designed by renowned architect Addison Mizner in 1992, in the Mediterranean Revival-Spanish Colonial Revival styles. Sensitively preserved and converted to a condominium in the 1980s - a fine example of adaptive-reuse.
National Registry of Historic Places

William Gray Warden House
112 Seminole Avenue

The Lido-Venice was built in 1928 and renamed **The Vineta Hotel.** In 1937, it was renovated by architect John L. Volk and renamed The Chesterfield, a member of the Red Carnation Hotel Collection and Small Luxury Hotels of the World in 1989. *National Registry of Historic Places*

Vineta Hotel *(Chesterfield Hotel)*
363 Cocoanut Row

The **Bradley Park Hotel** has its architecture based on Mediterranean Revival style with a fountain, and arched entryways. It still stands on the same historic location since the early 1920s.

Bradley Park Hotel
280 Sunset Avenue

The Colony Hotel
155 Hammon Avenue

"It has served as host to presidents, royalty and celebrities over its 67 years and has maintained its special aura to this day. Once painted purple and featuring a Florida-shaped pool, the **Colony** has been transformed again by the 2014 renovations under the guidance of Carleton Varney.

In addition to its well-known hospitality, the Colony has received wide acclaim for its entertainment venue, the Royal Room. Cabaret is alive and well in Palm Beach thanks to the talented ears of Rob Russell and Roger Everingham who travel the country to find the newest talent – established entertainers cannot wait to return to the intimate setting and connection to Worth Avenue. In years past, there was a well-worn path between the hotel and Ta-boo – the stars were out and the Colony served as their host." *Courtesy of Palm Beach Daily News*

Easter Fashion Show at the Biltmore Hotel

1925 - **The Alba Hotel** was opened, located on the Intercoastal Waterway and Bradley Place. It was later named the **Palm Beach Biltmore Hotel.**

The hotel was converted into condominiums by architect Eugene Lawrence in 1970. It is a unique mix of traditional old world elegance, gracious marble foyers and high ceilings together with modern amenities.

The Biltmore Condominiums, 150 Bradley Place

The Brazillian Court Hotel, 301 Australian Avenue

1926 - **The Brazilian Court Hote**l opened New Year's Day. It was designed by Sicilian born, New York architect, Rosario Candela. He developed the Mediterranean-style design around an inner courtyard, with tiled roofs and stucco. It was originally an apartment hotel with guest room kitchenettes. In 2013 under new ownership, it was re-developed with a cosmopolitan style. The guest room kitchenettes were removed and a restaurant added, Café Boulud with renowned NY Chef Daniel Boulud.

Aerial view of the Brazillian Court Hotel

Huntington, Anna Hyatt (1876-1973) U.S.A.
"The Passing of the Torch, 1953" Aluminum

Silver King 1988 by D.H.S Wehle,
American 1951

Grainger McKoy (1947-) American
Recovery 2010, Stainless Steel, ed. 2

The **Society of the Four Arts**, on Royal Palm Way was founded in 1936. The Plaza's original building was designed by architect Maurice Fatio and now houses a library. Architect Addison Mizner designed the building, which includes the Esther B. O'Keeffe Art Gallery, a concert hall auditorium, two libraries and an administration building.

In 1938 the Demonstration Gardens were established and maintained by the Garden Club of Palm Beach. These gardens display: tropical plants, a Chinese garden, a moongate and statuary, with a pathway winding past a rock garden, a Spanish facade and decorative wall. There are large trees that shade the way to the Madonna Garden and a formal fountain.

Library Entrance - Society of the Four Arts

Society of the Four Arts - Plaza and Fountain

The Society of the Four Arts

Society of the Four Arts - Chinese Garden

Palm Beach Private Clubs

The Bath and Tennis Club, *Courtesy of Frank Coniglio's collection*

...as the Palm Beach community grew, so did their social life - from hotels to private clubs.

E.R. Bradleys Beach Club, *Courtesy of Frank Coniglio's collection*

"When Col Edward Riley "E.R." Bradley died in 1946, Joe Kennedy uttered his famous lament: "Palm Beach has lost its zipperoo." And few would have argued. Earning his fortune through horse breeding and racing, Bradley, with his brother, John, opened the private Beach Club in 1898 – but it has little to do with the beach. Instead, the club offered high-stakes gambling for the well-to-do – illegal, of course. But authorities regularly turned a blind eye toward the exclusive establishment that banned locals – only seasonal visitors were admitted – and listed on prices on the dinner menu. E.R. Bradley, who once owned The Palm Beach Post, was generous to Palm Beach, largely funding the construction of St. Edward Catholic Church with his brother. He closed the Beach Club in 1945 and willed it to the town with the provision that it be torn down and the land become a park. An original wall from his house stands in Bradley Park as a silent memorial to a man who even by Palm Beach standards lived an extraordinarily large life."
Courtesy of Palm Beach Daily News

PHOTO CREDIT: Bob Davidoff

1914 - **The Sailfish Club** is one of the oldest remaining private clubs in Palm Beach. It met at The Breakers Casino for many years. In 1932 the Sailfish Club of Palm Beach joined with the Palm Beach Anglers and Sports Clubs to become the Sailfish Club of Florida. They built a clubhouse and pier on North Lake Way two years later.

1926 - Joseph Urban designed the **Bath and Tennis Club** as an athletic and social club. Urban was also a set designer and produced elaborate sets for parties at private homes.

1918 - **The Everglades Club:** Paris Singer together with his friend, the architect Addison Mizner (1872-1933), decided that they would build a hospital. This was during World War I and at a time when only war related buildings could be built. Singer had already built three hospitals in France. However, the war ended prior to the building's completion, resulting in its conversion into a private club.

1919 - **The Everglades Club** began with twenty-five charter members with Paris Singer as the club President (Singer's father, Isaac Singer was the inventor of the sewing machine). In 1920, the club had additions of: a nine hole golf course; eleven apartments and sixteen shops. This development was after an interesting historical start.

The Everglades Club, *courtesy of Frank Coniglio's collection*

The Palm Beach Country Club (original building)

1917 - The (members-only) **Palm Beach Country Club** opened. Located at 760 Ocean Blvd, this is a country club and golf facility. The original structure is featured here, courtesy of the Tallahassee, Florida Archives. It has since re-built.

The Club is bordered by Atlantic Ocean to the east and intercoastal to the west. It is an 18-hole facility in Palm Beach, Florida. It was designed by Donald J. Ross, ASGCA. The course rating is 72.1 with a slope rating of 118. Palm Beach is a private equity facility golf course with a 'Accompanied By Member' guest policy. *Source: Golf Link and Golf Now.*

1941 - The (members-only) **Beach Club** was built by well-known resorter, Jack Mitchell. Originally known as the **Coral Beach Club,** designed by John Volk, a young Austrian architect. Jack Mitchell operated the club for three decades. It was famous for its private parties and was one of the first clubs to be called friendly.
Mitchell's well-known quote of the time was, "Gentlemen, it's time for a change. You'll have to start wearing shoes on the dance floor." The gentlemen protested, refusing to wear socks with their shoes, thus starting a new Palm Beach tradition.

Jack Mitchell sold the club to a group of men known as "The Founders" in 1969. The old Coral Beach Club structure was demolished, with the new clubhouse was once again designed by John Volk. The new Beach Club opened its doors in 1970 and became known as "The Club for All Seasons," since it remained open for eleven months of the year with a reciprocal arrangement with the Sailfish Club for the twelfth month. It is located at the same North-end site on North Ocean Boulevard and North County Road (755 N. County Rd). *Source information - www.thebeachclub.net*

1995: Mar-a-Lago was transformed into the Mar-a-Lago Club by Donald J. Trump

Mar-a-Lago (from ocean to lake)

by Laurel Baker

This fabled national landmark, built in 1927, sits on 17 acres of ocean to lake property. The 122-room house has 55,695 square feet of living space – a fantasy beyond a Hollywood stage set and the realization of a dream by Marjorie Merriweather Post – Hutton. Married to E. F. Hutton at the time – he listened and Mar-a-Lago rose.

It was a palace – opulent, regal, stately and so very over the top in its furnishings. There was an Art Deco room in part of the tower to diffuse the richness. Designed by Marion Syms Wyeth and Joseph Urban, the house was a dramatic illusion.

While many of the decorative features such as the wrought iron, doors and beams were made locally, the house itself was an international clearing house with materials and artisans from Italy, Spain, Portugal, Austria, England and Holland.

Mrs. Post was crowned the "Queen of Palm Beach" and conducted her affairs accordingly. Entertaining lavishly, bringing great celebrities of the day to visit and sponsoring a variety of charity events, Mar-a-Lago became the epitome of style and grace – few, if any, could match.

The house was given to the federal government upon her death in 1973; however, finding the estate too costly and too difficult to secure were the president or foreign dignitaries to visit, the property was sold. It sat empty for years, until the knight in shining armor saved the day – and the property – in 1985.

Donald J. and Melania Trump

Today, Donald Trump's Mar-a-Lago echoes the refrains of Mrs. Post's lavish, much sought-after lifestyle. Operating as a private club, the events rival those of the 30s and 40s with the food, festivities, guests and celebrities. Few could accomplish such a feat today – save for Marjorie Merriweather Post and Donald Trump.

Left top: Aerial photograph of Mar-a-Lago property, ocean to lake, photographed by Robert Davidoff.
Bottom left: Photo: State Archives of Florida, Florida Memory, http://floridamemory.com, FM # 76687 Mrs. Meriweather Post
Bottom Right: A Costume Dinner Party on the Patio of Mar-a-Lago, Courtesy of Marjorie Merriweather Post
Vintage Photo (faded in background) State Archives of Florida, Florida Memory, http://floridamemory.com

PHOTO CREDIT: Devine

Little Known...

The Kapok tree on the grounds of the Royal Poinciana Chapel next to the Lake Trail bike trail bears an interesting history. Originally planted by the Garden Supervisor at Flagler's Royal Poinciana Hotel. The Champion Tree survived numerous hurricanes, has provided a picturesque setting for many weddings and provides shade to many a pensive soul resting on the bike trail or, reading under it's branches.

The Kapok tree also bears religious beliefs in some cultures. The Mayans considered it to be very sacred. The souls of the dead had to reach the top branches to reach heaven. In some African cultures sleeping on a Kapok pillow is believed to purify the soul and allows new energy to flow through ones body. Today, Kapok is used to make lifejackets and lifebuoys. It is a very buoyant substance and does not absorb water. The Kapok tree grows wild in the subtropical and tropical climate zones, and can grow up to 100 m high with an approximate lifetime of 300 years.

Kapok tree and bike trail

Worth Avenue stretches across four blocks between Lake Worth and the Atlantic Ocean. There are unique European-styled vias off the avenue where people live and shop. These vias distinguish Worth Avenue from many other shopping experiences.

PHOTO: State Archives of Florida, Florida Memory, http://floridamemory.com

Fortune Publication 1936

Worth Avenue, *Courtesy of Frank Coniglio's collection*

Via Mizner, Worth Avenue – designed by Addison Mizner. *The National Registry of Historic Places.*

The Vias

A Palm Beach Legacy of European Elegance

by Laurel Baker

Just what is a via [long e-sound] – and why are they so special? When Addison Mizner came to town and began development of Worth Avenue as an early example of today's 'new urbanism', he took images from his many travels around the world and created a magical experience that would encourage visitors to wander and enjoy – and perhaps discover romance, intrigue and happiness. Mizner introduced the development concept of mixed use – having business, residential and commercial enterprises grouped together. Worth Avenue was a forerunner – and integral to that development were vias.

A route, a diversion, a thoroughfare, an alleé – but, please do not call them alleys! Mizner's vias had specific characteristics, but each via had its own unique personality. A via will have angels, chandeliers, a water feature, lush planting and wrought-iron gates or ornamentation, statuary and tile work, staircases and a mix of facades lending a more continental air to the setting.

1911 to 1925 represented the heyday of development on Palm Beach, much of the credit going to that imaginative Californian, Addison Mizner. His break with conventional architecture on the island's Florida vernacular style transformed Palm Beach into a larger than life stage set of over the top houses and commercial growth. Transforming an alligator pond to a fairytale palace with the Everglades Club, the avenue acquired a lively rhythm that reverberated across the globe. Mizner Industries evolved from Worth Avenue – eventually producing the wrought-iron, tiles and lamps and furnishings that were distinctively Mizner.

With the exception of vias Mizner and Parigi, the vias did not have names until much later, often assuming the moniker of the nearby business. Explore the avenue and experience the unique personality of each of the vias – create your own story to capture the memories.

VIA MIZNER – "grandness" with three distinct areas, this first via was all Mizner – not only in name, but in grandeur. The original layout included 19 buildings housing forty small shops. A five-storey apartment complex was added for Mizner's personal use. His office, accessible via a bridge over middle archway leading to Renato's al fresco dining delight. A courtyard filled with bougainvillea adds romance to any visit.

Via Amoré

Via Parigi

Via Demario

l-r: Aldo Gucci, Miss Universe Rena Messenger and Jesse Newman

"Jesse Newman, a former Worth Avenue retailer who served as president of the Palm Beach Chamber for 29 years beginning in the early 1970s; his unabashed promotion of the town earned him an honorary title: "Mr. Palm Beach." *Courtesy of Palm Beach Daily News*

PHOTO CREDIT: Bob Davidoff

Jim Peterson, who owned Ta-boó with Marshall Grant, society band leader

"Ta-boo' restaurant and lounge opens, just days before the United States enters World War II on December 7." *Courtesy of Palm Beach Daily News*

Worth

French for 'little pot,' **Petite Marmite** was actually a melting pot of sorts, attracting diners at one time or another from just about every strata of Palm Beach society. A regular dining spot for some and a 'special-occasion' spot for others, the restaurant opened on Worth Avenue in 1949 and remained an island mainstay for decades. The owners, Gus and Gerri Pucillo, understood their clientele perfectly, offering fine French and Italian cuisine that pleased the palates of patrons that included King Hussein of Jordan, Emily Post, members of the Kennedy clan, Liberace and the Duke and Duchess of Windsor.

PHOTO CREDIT: Devine

Artist Andy Warhol

Actress Anne Margaret

Queen Alia Hussein and King Hussein on Worth Avenue

Worth Avenue 2011 Redesign

"In a precedent-setting collaboration of efforts, the property owners of Worth Avenue collectively partnered to breathe new life into the hardscape and landscape of this world-renowned shopping destination."
Robin Miller, General Manager of The Worth Avenue Association.
Courtesy of Devine Palm Beach Centennial Issue.

Breaking Ground – Worth Avenue Redesign
Left to right: Town Council President David Rosow, Town Councilman Bill Diamond, The Honorable Mayor Gail Coniglio, Property Owner Burt Handelsman, Property Owner/Merchant Ed Kassatly, Attorney/Historian Harvey Oyer III, Town Councilman Richard Kleid, Leslie Shaw, (former Town Councilman) Serge Lefavre, Architect Mark Marsh, Deputy Town Manager Tom Bradford, Palm Beach Historian James Ponce, (former Mayor) Jack McDonald, Worth Ave Association President Sherry Frankel.

The Palm Beach Centennial
1911-2011

PHOTO CREDIT: Lucien Capehart

The Palm Beach Centennial 1911 - 2011

Palm Beach, a small town of international renown, occupies a mere slip of land, less than 16 miles long and one mile wide on the 'gold coast' of Florida's east coast. It began its notable history a mere swampland, first appealing to hunters and fishermen. It all changed when a corporate visionary brought his railroad to Florida – and to his hotels. With private railcars bringing northeastern society to Palm Beach, its social position grew. The houses – grand estates rose from the swampland. Elegance beyond imagination took hold. By the end of World War II, permanent residents established a small but mighty town that remains a much-sought after destination which has appealed to titans of industries and philanthropists around the globe. With such an audience, celebrating the town's 100th Anniversary was guaranteed to be grand.

Troy and Olympia Devine PR/Event Coordinators

The Palm Beach Centennial at The Mar-a-Lago Club

Friday April 15 to Sunday 17, 2011
No one could have imagined a more outstanding weekend of celebrations to recognize the official incorporation of the Town of Palm Beach. Festivities large and small added up to a spectacular observance of a spectacular community.

PHOTO CREDIT: Lucien Capehart

Hosted by Donald Trump, the official Centennial Opening Night Cocktail Reception welcomed 1,000 guests and club members to the legendary home of Marjorie Merriweather Post. Mr. Trump commented during the press conference while the party was in full swing that the event was "…probably the best party we ever had at Mar-a-Lago."

The Palm Beach Centennial at The Breakers

Saturday, April 16th at The Breakers Palm Beach
What more fitting locale to honor the Centennial Ambassadors than at The Breakers Palm Beach – Henry Flagler's landmark hotel. For complete accuracy, even the menu was chosen from the archives of 1911 and included caviar, lobster poached in champagne, Beef Wellington and coconut crème brulée. Hotel CEO and President, Paul Leone, described the evening's event as one of the most extraordinary affairs in the hotel's history, rivaling the dinner held when the hotel was awarded the prestigious Mobile 5 Diamond Award. The guests gathered for the evening paid tribute to those exceptional individuals in the community for their tireless efforts to protect and preserve the social, economic and philanthropic endeavors that have distinguished Palm Beach.

PHOTO CREDIT: Lucien Capehart

The Centennial Ambassadors were chosen for recognition during the Centennial for their outstanding contributions to the Town of Palm Beach through leadership, philanthropy, civic responsibility and professional standards of excellence in business, charitable giving and the arts.

Centennial Ambassadors

Mr. James Y. Arnold, Jr.
Mrs. Lillian Fanjul De Azqueta
Mrs. Kenyon C. Bolton
Mrs. Helen S. Cluett
Mrs. F. Eugene Dixon, Jr.
Mr. Alexander W. Dreyfoos
Hon. Ambassador Edward E. Elson
Mr. Alfonso Fanjul
Mr. J. Pepe Fanjul
Dame Celia Lipton Farris
Mrs. Marjorie S. Fisher
Mrs. Jane R. Grace
Mr. Robert M. Grace
Dr. Robert Green
Mrs. Diana B.B. Holt
Mrs. Frances A. Hufty
Mrs. Philip Hulitar
Mr. Edward M. Kassatly
Mr. Thomas S. Kenan
Mr. Sidney A. Kohl
Mr. Leonard A Lauder
Mrs. Elsie G. Leviton
Mr. H. Irwin Levy
Mr. Paul L. Maddock, Jr.
Mr. Morton L. Mandel
Mr. George G. Matthews
Mr. William M. Matthews
Mrs. John R. McLean
Mr. Ogden Mills Phipps
Mr. David V. Reese
Mrs. Wiley R. Reynolds
Mrs. Barbara M. Rogers
Mr. Doyle Rogers
Dr. Saul D. Rotter
Mrs. Lillian Lee Pulitzer Rousseau
Mr. Stanley Rumbough, Jr.
Mrs. Kathryn Rybovich
Mrs. Rose Sachs
The Honorable Lesly S. Smith
Dr. Donald E. Warren
Mrs. Betty Anne Warren
Mr. Floyd L. Wideman, Jr.

The Palm Beach Centennial at The Flagler Museum

Sunday, April 17th: What is a town celebration without a parade? In anticipation of the grand party on the green at Henry Flagler's historic home, citizens, children, businesses and service groups gathered on the playing field of the Palm Beach Day Academy and paraded on to the Flagler. Hometown favorites like Lilly Pulitzer and her family, Mayor Gail Coniglio, town council members and staff waved to the crowds from a variety of antique cars owned by Palm Beachers and shared for the evening.

Then a hush fell over the crowd as the most incredible show was about to begin: this was the premiere presentation of a 'sound and light' show with 3-D image mapping projected onto the front façade of Whitehall. Words cannot begin to describe the magical show filled with ever-changing images of cocoanuts, trains, dancing ladies and dapper gentlemen. There was more magic with fireworks over the Lake Worth Inlet, synchronized to the memorable music of Tchaikovsky's 1812 Overture.

The Parade

PHOTO CREDIT: Jeffrey Langolis courtesty of Palm Beach Daily News

ALL PHOTOS ABOVE, CREDIT: Lucien Capehart

Gathered on the grand marble stairway to Whitehall, joining town officials were (l - r) George Matthews, Governor Rick Scott, Mayor Gail Coniglio and Congressman Allen West. Behind them, the 100 angelic voices of the Young Singers of the Palm Beaches led the crowd of over 4000 in singing Happy Birthday to a much beloved town.

The Flagler Museum on night of the Centennial Celebration

The Palm Beach Centennial

Event Chairs, Board of Directors and Executive Committee

Top Row: Howard and Michele Kessler, David Koch, Bill Koch, Bobbi and Harry Horwich M.D.; Middle Row: Bill Metzger-Director, Alec and Miriam Flamm, Tom Quick, Peggy and Dudley Moore, Kathryn and Leo Vecellio, Talbott Maxey, Laurel Baker-Director; Front Row: Cynthia Friedman-Secretary, Edward Elson-Vice Chair, Bill Bone-Chairman, Betsy Matthews-Vice Chair, Kevin A. Johnson-Treasurer.

The Palm Beach Centennial Commission

Mr. Bill Bone *Chairman*
Amb.Edward E. Elson *Vice Chair*
Mrs. Betsy Matthews *Vice Chair*
Mr. Kevin Johnson *Treasurer*
Ms. Cynthia Friedman *Secretary*
Mr. Ervin S. Duggan *Director*
Mr. Bill Metzger *Director*
Ms. Laurel Baker *Director*
Mr. Jay Boodheshwar *Advisor*

Mr. John Blades
Ms. Joyce Cohen
Ms. Sherry Frankel
Ms Isabel Furlaud
Mr. Edward Kassatly
The Honorable Richard Kleid
Mr. Daniel McDonnell
Ms. Pamela McIver

Mr. Zach Morfogen
Ms Debbie Murray
Ms. Janice Owens
Ms. Susan Polan
Mr. Jimmy Ryan
Ms. Patricia L. Sans
Mrs. Sharon Stewart Neri

Ambassadors' Sketches

The Centennial Ambassadors were chosen for their outstanding contributions to the Town of Palm Beach through leadership, philanthropy, civic responsibility and professional standards of excellence in business, charitable giving and the arts.

PHOTO CREDIT: Palm Beach Daily News

James Y. Arnold, Jr.
A Palm Beach pioneer who has lived on the hill overlooking the Intracoastal Waterway for decades, Jim's enthusiasm for life and the character of the town is unmatched. The family's ties to the island remain strong, with grandchildren carrying on the Arnolds' love affair with Palm Beach.

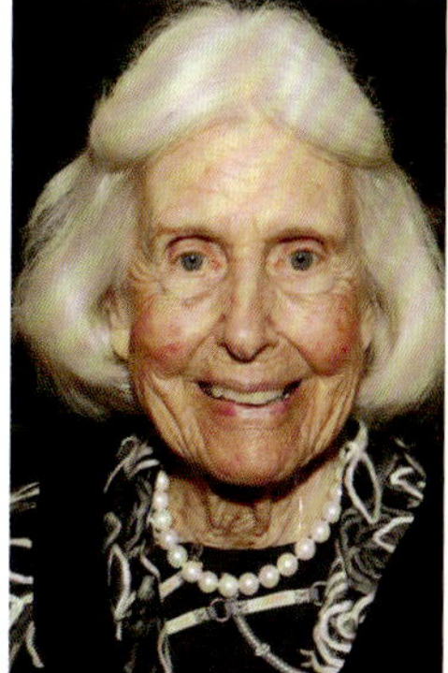

Mary Bolton
She and her family laid their roots on Palm Beach in 1893 when her grandfather, Charles W. Bingham, built the first oceanfront house. Family pride of place led Mrs. Bolton's son, Kenyon "Tim" Bolton, an award-winning architect, to design and build Figulus III and Figulus IV on the family property. She has been a long-time member of The Garden Club of Palm Beach.

Helen S. Cluett
She came to Palm Beach in 1959. Her commitment to family, church and community has distinguished her as a leader. Her board and event chair services to non-profits including Opportunity, Inc., the Episcopal Church of Bethesda-by-the-Sea, the Palm Beach Chamber, the Fellowship of Christians and Jews and the Historical Society set a standard for excellence.

Edith 'Edie' Dixon
Edie Dixon has led by example, directing her energies to systematic problem-solving and efficient actions. She has not merely carried on the Fitz Dixon legacy, but added a greater strength to the goals envisioned by institutions such as The Society of the Four Arts, a legacy that is a testament to her many talents.

Alexander W. Dreyfoos
He was the force behind the creation of the Kravis as a performing arts center, the growth of the Dreyfoos School of the Arts, the advancement of the sciences as the future industry in Palm Beach County with his involvement with the Scripps and Max Planck research institutions. The Cultural Council for the Palm Beach County was established by him – and has made the area the leading cultural center for the arts in the state.

Ambassador Edward E. Elson
After serving as Rector of the University of Virginia and first chairman of NPR and its Foundation, Ed was appointed Ambassador to Denmark from 1993 to 1998. His diplomatic skills, coupled with his artistic sensitivities, have greatly benefited both the Society for the Four Arts and the Preservation Foundation of Palm Beach.

Lillian 'Lian' Fanjul de Azqueta
Beyond the title 'First Family of Florida Sugar', the Fanjul family reflects the passion, compassion and support that is a matchless template for others to achieve. The Fanjuls take pride in their history and the future they have built as leaders in the community. Lillian Fanjul de Azqueta founded two non-profit organizations, New Hope Charities and the MIR Foundation (Mission International Rescue Charities) in the Dominican Republic.

Alfonso 'Alfy' Fanjul Jr.
For over a century, the Fanjul family has been identified with the sugar industry. The emphasis on family ties is a mark of the successes realized over the past century and a half. Alfonso Fanjul serves as the chairman and CEO of Fanjul Corp and Florida Crystals Corp. He has supported numerous charitable and educational organizations and co-founded the MIR Foundation (Mission International Rescue Charities) in the Dominican Republic.

Jose 'Pepe' Fanjul
Jose Fanjul serves as the vice chairman and CEO of Fanjul Corp. and Florida Crystals Corp. both sugar production companies. The Fanjul family's support of charitable and educational initiatives is the hallmark of the response to the pressing needs of others. Jose is the chairman of New Hope Charities founded by Lillian Fanjul de Azqueta.

Dame Celia Lipton Farris
Born in England, Dame Farris captured the world's heart through the theatre. As Peter Pan, she rose to international prominence with her singing, painting and humanitarian efforts. There were few charities that did not benefit from her generosity over the years. Most notable: the Victor Farris Pavilion at Good Samaritan Hospital, given to honor her late husband, Victor; the Kravis Center and AIDS research. Her generosity continues through the Farris Foundation.

Marjorie S. Fisher
Along with her late husband, Max Fisher, Marjorie has cast a wide net in the community through their philanthropic efforts to better the lives of children. Most notably, the dedication of the Boys & Girls Club facilities in Riviera Beach, named for Max Fisher, marked one of the most significant community gifts for the future.

Robert M. Grace and Jane R. Grace
Individually and as a couple, Bob and Jane Grace are the standard bearers of true citizens. Their tireless efforts to preserve, protect and propagate all that is good about Palm Beach have touched every aspect of life on the island. Leadership, through government service, the Society of the Four Arts, Preservation and animal rescue has enriched the community and served as an unparalleled example of selfless dedication.

Dr. Robert Green
With compassion, wit and skill, Dr. Green has represented the best of Palm Beach as physician, friend and observer of the light and lively side of Palm Beach. When his father and uncle opened the ever-popular Green's Pharmacy, he gained even greater insight on the ways of the island.

Diana B. Holt
Scholar, adventurer, inveterate wit, and champion bridge player, Diana Holt has traveled the world, pursuing her lifetime interest in the archeological projects in China and East Africa. Her world view impacted her charitable giving to support the needs of medicine, science, mental health and rehabilitation.

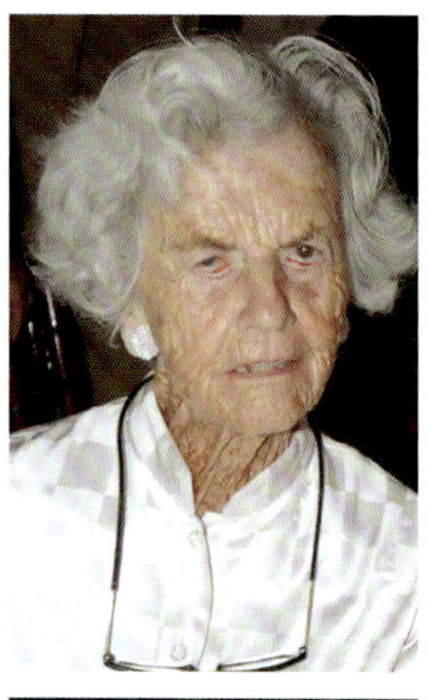

Frances A. Hufty
She was an early proponent of environmental causes and conservation efforts. Two noteworthy endeavors include the Archibold Biological Station and the Pine Jog Environmental Education Center. As her daughter, Page Lee Hufty noted during the centennial year, "We share an island graced by the legacy of inspired architects and amateur gardeners – a place where constantly surprising floral and bird life keep us tropical folks endlessly bewitched and amused."

Mary Hulitar
The Hulitars were an exceptional couple as leaders in Palm Beach. Blending the talents of a prominent American couturier with a public-spirited individual, Philip and Mary Hulitar contributed an unmatched focus on beauty. The sculpture gardens at the Society of the Fours Arts are a tribute to Philip's artistic talents as well as their mutual appreciation of Palm Beach. Completed in 1980, the gardens are a timeless gift to the community.

Edward M. Kassatly
"For 90 years, there's always been a Kassatly's. Sam and Alice Kassatly first opened a seasonal linens shop on the island with another store on Long Island's East End in 1923, ...The family's first Palm Beach store was in the Beaux Arts shopping center on Bradley Place, but a few years later, it moved to the then-newly established Worth Avenue commercial stretch..." - *Courtesy of Palm Beach Daily News*

Thomas S. Kenan, III
As a descendent of Mary Lily Kenan Flagler (wife of Henry M. Flagler), Thomas continues the Flagler legacy and the institutions that fortify Palm Beach, Tom Kenan's engagement with Flagler Systems and the Flagler Museum reflect his loyalty and concern for future generations. This commitment is furthered at the University of North Carolina at Chapel Hill.

Sidney A. and Dorothy Kohl
With Midwest sensibilities and international flair, the Kohls have established themselves as arbiters of style and artistic renowned. Their leadership on various boards within Palm Beach and the greater community, from social services to the arts and to medicine, has generously enriched many lives.

Leonard A. Lauder
Recognized as one of the country's leading businessmen, Leonard and family are valued threads in the Palm Beach tapestry. He is the son of Estee Lauder (renowned cosmetic business leader). He is the chairman of Estee Lauder Co. The value of family and the family name are reflected in the many charitable efforts supported over the years.

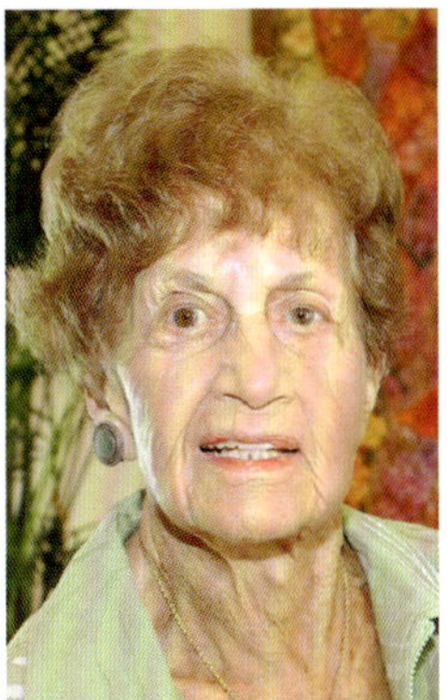

Elsie G. Leviton
An outstanding example of the modern woman focused on relevant issues related to health, education and human services, Elsie and her late husband, Dr. Lawrence Leviton, have served as beacons for countless individuals in the county.

H. Irwin Levy
Innovator, humanitarian and family-oriented, Irwin was an early developer of Century Village. An attorney by trade, he has devoted himself to Jewish causes, both in the States and abroad, a tradition begun by his mother and now carried out by his son.

Paul L. Maddock, Jr.
Jay Maddock's family knows Palm Beach well, having built 'Duck's Nest', an 1891 house that sat on property stretching from the ocean to the lake. The house, now landmarked, stands as a proud reminder of simpler times, fortitude and dignity.

Morton L. Mandel
For over half a century, Morton Mandel has called Palm Beach home, while remaining faithful to his hometown, Cleveland. Through his foundation, he has enriched the Palm Beach area through his support of many Jewish causes in the county along with his generous gift to the West Palm Beach Public Library, named in his honor.

William M. Matthews

As an heir to the Flagler legacy on Palm Beach, Will Matthews has carried on the traditions set by his ancestors through his involvement with the community. He is the son of Henry M. Flagler's granddaughter, Jean Flagler Matthews. In addition to his services to the Palm Beach Day Academy, Eaglebrook School, the Four Arts and the Community Foundation, he plays an active role in the Keenan Flagler Business School at the University of North Carolina at Chapel Hill.

George G. Matthews

As Henry Flagler's great-grandson, George Matthews has carried on the family interests in real estate and commercial investments. His tireless efforts to realize his mother's pledge to restore Whitehall as an historic house museum were realized. Town service as a member of the town council for sixteen years, eight as council president, further testify to a man committed to family and community.

Mildred Brown 'Brownie' McLean

With an indomitable spirit and a smile that is brighter than the Hope Diamond, Mildred Brown "Brownie" McLean is a national treasure. Indeed, who needed the Hope Diamond, actually owned by her in-laws, when you are Brownie? Her charitable endeavors have an international reach, including the Global Futures Foundation. Honored by numerous organizations for her tireless efforts on their behalf, including the American Red Cross.

Ogden Mills 'Dinny' Phipps

Dinny Phipps is another fourth-generation Palm Beacher, continues the family tradition and love of horses, breeding champions and the recognition and respect of his peers in the racing industry. The Phipps family created a legacy of commitment to community and family. Their generosity in providing land to Palm Beach and West Palm Beach for the perpetual enjoyment by many distinguishes their imprint on the future. Development of parcels such as the Poinciana Plaza and later Phipps Estates demonstrated an understanding of changing times and adaptation.

David R. Reese

He carries on the spirit of adventure and leadership set by his family which settled on Palm Beach in 1876. This has been a family of firsts – with "Cap" Dimick, David's great-grandfather, serving as the town's first mayor, opened the first bank. "Cap" Dimick is the first 'person' you see when crossing the middle bridge onto the island.

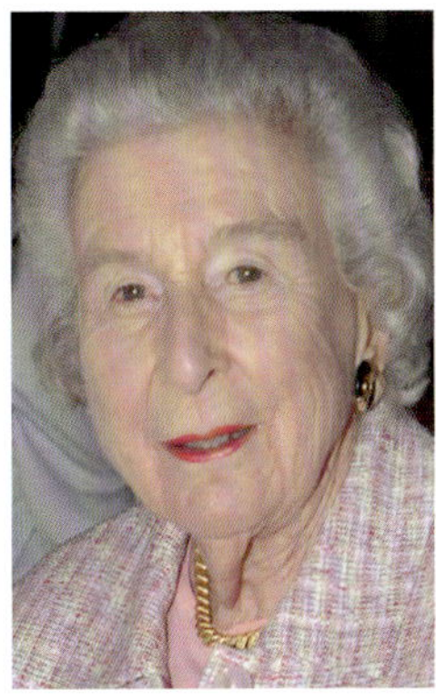

Janet Reynolds
The history of Palm Beach could not be complete without the inclusion of the Reynolds Family and their countless contributions to the growth and development of the town. With landmark memories seen in the First National Bank of Palm Beach building, Janet has continued in the remarkable heritage with the Rehabilitation Center for Children and Adults, along with the Norton Museum of Art, the Society of the Four Arts and newer social service agencies.

Doyle and Barbara M. Rogers
Whether dealing with issues of faith or public policy, Doyle's perspective has been sought and respected for generations. Joining her husband, Barbara has led by example in the support of tradition-bound island institutions such as the Society of the Four Arts and agencies such as the Town of Palm Beach United Way and the Community Foundation to meet the unmet needs.

Dr. Saul D. Rotter
With a medical career spanning six decades, Dr. Rotter's contributions to the Rehabilitation Center for Children and Adults are unsurpassed. Kindness, compassion and an astute eye to the ever-changing demands has distinguished his career and contributions to society.

Lillian 'Lilly' Pulitzer Rousseau
Born to a legendary family, Lilly Pulitzer Rousseau would become the first-name-only lady of fashion. Playful designs and brilliant colors combined to launch the "Palm Beach Look" – casual, slightly sassy and ever so practical: her first goal was to hide juice stains on her clothes while working at her Via Mizner juice stand. The rest is history.

Stanley M. Rumbough, Jr.
Entrepreneur, sportsman, scholar, leader and the person everyone wants to be with, Stan Rumbough has led by example, shared his insights without imposing his views, seeking comprise and right actions. His tenure as chairman of the Civic Association served the citizens of Palm Beach well and opened doors of opportunity for better dialogue.

Kathryn Rybovich
A love of fishing and conversation distinguish Kay Rybovich – and spinning a tale is among her many talents. Her love of people and this area have endeared her to many for her great ability to share history. She has made history as well, having been inducted into the International Game-fishing Hall of Fame

Rose Sachs
Considered the "Queen of Worth Avenue", Rose Sachs shared her love of the island and the extraordinary treasure of Worth Avenue with all. Having arrived in Palm Beach in the early 1940's she has been a landlord and witness to the extraordinary legacies of the town, its people and the architecture that has evolved.

The Honorable Lesly S. Smith
Wife to an ambassador, philanthropist and former town council member and mayor, Lesly's astute observations and natural curiosity have created a legacy for Palm Beach that few could match. As a political force, her leadership of the town through its strong periods of growth showed an understanding of urban redevelopment and civic responsibility. Lesly is a long-time member of The Garden Club of Palm Beach.

Dr. Donald E. and Betty Anne 'Bebe' Warren
Beloved cardiologist and community leader, Dr. Warren was instrumental in the early development of Palm Beach Atlantic University and its growth over the past four decades. Betty Anne 'Bebe' Warren was at Dr. Warren's side, watching the growth of Palm Beach Atlantic University. She founded the "Women of Distinction Award" to give recognition to the extraordinary contributions of women.

Floyd L. Wideman, Jr.
Passionate about Palm Beach, its history, heritage and architecture, Floyd has been a long-serving member of various town commissions dedicated to the preservation of Palm Beach. His most recent effort took advantage of his many talents as businessman and volunteer in the development of the Par 3 Golf Course.

The Legend Continues...

It took nearly a century, but Henry M. Flagler made it back to Palm Beach on December 12, 2010. The Henry M. Flagler statue presentation marked the kick-off of the Palm Beach Centennial Celebration. Mr. Flagler welcomes all who cross the north bridge at the westernmost median of Royal Poinciana Way.

The Legend Continues...

Flagler first arrived in Palm Beach in 1893. His Florida East Coast Railway led to the development of several Florida cities—St. Augustine, West Palm Beach, Miami and Key West. But, the most magical city of all was Palm Beach.

Despite discovering an island primarily filled with scrub and swamp, Flagler envisioned what it could be. He was helped in that vision by the exotic groves of coconut palms planted by the settlers after the shipwreck of the Providencia in 1878. Imagine what Florida might have been had Flagler not set his sights on making Palm Beach the "Queen of Winter Resorts"?

It took nearly a century, but Henry M. Flagler made it back to Palm Beach on December 12, 2010.

The presentation of a statue of Henry M. Flagler marked the kick-off of the Palm Beach Centennial Celebration. Standing 11-feet tall on a granite pedestal, Mr. Flagler welcomes all who cross the north bridge at the westernmost median of Royal Poinciana Way.

Family and friends gathered at Bradley Park for the unveiling of the statue. Col. G.F. Robert Hanke presented the statue as a gift to the town on behalf of the Flagler Museum. Hanke, Vice President of the Museum Trustees, generously funded the cost of reproducing and installing the bronze statue which was sculpted in Flagler's lifetime. Hanke discussed how Flagler's vision allowed Florida to flourish like no other state in the union. Even though Flagler died in 1913, his influence is as strong today as during the early 1900s.

PHOTO CREDIT: Lucien Capehart

Henry M. Flagler's descendents - The Flagler Museum Trustees: Col G F. Hanke, George Matthews and William Matthews

At the presentation ceremony, Palm Beach Centennial Commission Chairman, Bill Bone introduced Robert Hanke and briefly described his distinguished career: a retired Marine Corps Colonel who flew more than 175 combat missions in Vietnam and the Cuban missile crisis, a member of the Bar of the Court of Appeals of the Armed Forces and the U.S. Supreme Court, former Vice President and general counsel of The Asia Society and assistant to President Gerald Ford in Congress.

His military and Congressional decorations include the Distinguished Flying Cross, the Legion of Merit, the Navy and Marine Corps Medal for Heroism, the Air Medal with Silver Star and the Vietnamese Cross of Gallantry.

Like Flagler, who was helped by many in fulfilling his unique and special plans for Florida, the statue presentation was also a team effort.

PHOTO CREDIT: Lucien Capehart

John Blades, Museum Executive Director; Colonel G.F. Hanke and Bill Bone, Centennial Chairman.

The program was planned and executed by the Palm Beach Centennial Commission, Jay Boodheshwar, Town Director of Recreation, and John Blades, Executive Director of the Flagler Museum at Whitehall. Kevin Johnson, a senior manager of The Breakers Palm Beach was Treasurer of the Commission and Chairman of the Event Committee. Assisting him on the Committee were Ervin Duggan, President of the Society of Four Arts, Richard Kleid, Town Council Member and members of the residential and business communities.

The Mayor and Town Council were present at the unveiling, as were many of the men and women who had been named as Centennial Ambassadors. Ambassadors George Matthews, President of the Flagler Museum and his brother, William Matthews, Treasurer of the Museum, represented the new generation of Flagler heirs carrying on the traditions of excellence established by Henry Flagler.

Thanks to the support of Colonel Robert Hanke, the Matthews, the Carters, Hedrick Brothers Construction, Ray Celedinas and the Centennial Commission, thousands of Palm Beach residents and visitors will be greeted by the Town's visionary, Henry Flagler, as they arrive on the island by way of Flagler Memorial Bridge.

Centennial Notables

PHOTO CREDIT: Lucien Capehart

Bill Bone, Sylvia Hassenfeld, David and Bill Koch

Frank Coniglio and Mayor Gail Coniglio

Wendy Harrison and Peter Elwell

Senator Bill Nelson and Bobbi Horwich

John and Rena Blades

Kathryn and Leo Vecellio

Peggy and Dudley Moore

Miriam and Alec Flamm

Howard and Michele Kessler

George and Betsy Matthews

Bobbi and Dr. Harry Horwich

Talbott Maxey and Tom Quick

Angela and Congressman Allen West

Paul and Kathy Leone

Anne and Jay Boodheshwar

Centennial Notables

Ambassador Edward and Susie Elson

Jamie Pierce and Brad Deflin

(l-r) Debra LeVasseur, Susan Soares, Carolyn Rafaelian, Giovanni Feroce and Margo Madden

Marilyn and Zachary Morfogen

Eileen and Brian Burns

Sidney and Dorothy Kohl

Jose "Pepe" and Emilia Fanjul

Jana and John Scarpa

Orator and Maureen Woodward

Denise and William Meyer

Danielle Hickox Moore and Lesly Smith

Freuma and Dr. Elliott Klorfein

Bob Merril and Hillie Mahoney

Margi and Edward Allinson

Ambassador Nancy Brinker and Howard Bernick

Centennial Notables

Arlette and Robert "Bob" Gordon

Ray and Kim Celedenas
Jack and Cathy Flagg

Walter Ross

Mark and Mary Freitas

Bill and Kit Pannill

Bebe and Dr. Donald Warren

Jane Scott

Irwin and Ellen Levy

Mary Montgomery

Nancy and Don Carter

Kathryn and Rush Limbaugh

Cathy, Dale and Cheney Hedrick

Wilbur and Hillary Ross

Jeff Greene and Mayor Gail Coniglio

Robin and Richard S. Bernstein

Centennial Notables

Renate and Alex Dreyfoos

Sandra and David Mack

Hermé de Wyman Miro

(l-r) Jean and William Matthews, Lavina Baker and John McGruder

Bud Tamarkin and Rose Sachs

Lilly Pulitzer, Chris Leidy, Minnie McCluskey, Bobby Leidy, Lilly Leas, Liza Pulitzer and Bob Leidy

Kevin Lamb, Meike LeMieux, Senator George LeMieux, Karen Lamb

Karyn and Kevin Lamb

Doyle and Barbara Rogers

Town Councilman Dick Kleid

(l-r) Donald Trump, Mai Harrison and Hillie Mahoney

Alexander Ives and Laurel Baker

(l-r) Richard and Pat Johnson, Cathy and Jack Flagg

Lourdes Azqueta and Alfonso Fanjul

Cynthia Friedman

Little Known....

Palm Beach reaches its first century with a fun-filled, elegant and spectacular celebration! Even by Palm Beach standards this was a pretty good weekend for all Palm Beach residents as they celebrated the town's 1911 incorporation.

Palm Beach, Florida: Friday April 15 through Sunday 17, 2011.

Friday night, the private Mar-a-Lago Club and Mr. Donald Trump hosted the Centennial Opening Night Cocktail party. Mr. Trump held a press conference while the party was in progress to announce it was a record event group and 1,000 guests.

Saturday night, The Breakers Palm Beach hosted the Recognition and Thank You dinner for the Centennial Ambassadors (The Island's 1st families and residents with worldwide reputations who have a connection to Palm Beach for 50+ years) and Major Donors to the Centennial Celebration. The menu was taken from the archives of 1911 and included caviar, lobster poached in champagne, Beef Wellington and Coconut Crème Brulee... in a coconut.

PHOTO CREDIT: Lucien Capehart

Sunday at The Flagler Museum was the actual Centennial Celebration. The evening began with a parade of more than 1,200 participants promenading from the Palm Beach Day Academy to the Flagler Museum... Yes, there was a parade!

Then, almost exactly 100 years to the minute after Palm Beach was incorporated as a town, approximately 4,000 Palm Beach residents and friends sang Happy Birthday with Governor Rick Scott, Congressman Allen West, Palm Beach Mayor Gail Coniglio and the Town Council: David Rosow (President), Robert Wildrick (President pro tem), Bill Diamond, Dick Kleid, Michael Pucillo and Centennial Chairman, Bill Bone. Rounding out their voices were the 100 children of the famed Young Singers of the Palm Beaches.

A Palm Beach and South Florida first: Perhaps the most surprising part of the night was the premier presentation in South Florida of a jaw dropping "sound & light" show with 3-D image mapping projected onto the entire front facade of the Flagler Museum and ending with Tchaikovsky's 1812 Overture, synchronized with fireworks over Lake Worth.

Centennial Event Press Release: April 19, 2011.

Numerous smaller events (pre-April 2011) formed part of the Town's Centennial Celebrations. One of the more notable was the unveiling of the Henry M. Flagler Statue on December 12, 2010. This marked the kick-off of the Palm Beach Centennial celebrations. Standing 11-feet tall on a granite pedestal, Mr. Flagler welcomes all who cross the north bridge at the westernmost meridian of Royal Palm Way. This presentation event is described within the Centennial pages.

Another notable Palm Beach Centennial event was **Windows of Worth (WOW): January 22nd through March 5th, 2011.**

"... a caravan of vintage automobiles, with their horns-a-tootin', made its way down Worth Avenue Saturday afternoon to mark the finale of the Windows of Worth Centennial celebration.

Businesses along Worth Avenue, South County Road and Royal Poinciana Way were involved in the event, which included a window-display contest to salute the 100th Anniversary of the town's founding.

Mayor Gail Coniglio was among several community leaders and residents, some of whom were dressed in period costumes, who took part in the procession, which featured a trolley full of Palm Beach Day Academy fourth and fifth graders performing songs along the route."
Courtesy of Palm Beach Daily News, March 7th, 2011

Biba St. Croix with her fabulous winning Marilyn Monroe windows

Pascale DuWat Interieurs winning window

Patricia Reybold at the Windows of Worth parade

Palm Beach Mayor, Gail L. Coniglio

Frank Coniglio and Mayor Gail L. Coniglio at the Palm Beach Centennial

A few words from the Mayor of Palm Beach...

Palm Beach is a fully developed community, world-renowned for its extraordinary beauty, quality of life and small-town character. As we envision our future, we see Palm Beach remaining true to the inspired legacy of our founders, a Mediterranean-style Mecca of stunning architecture and natural beauty, acclaimed shopping, restaurants and hotels, a cosmopolitan culture, and an involved citizenry committed to civic and philanthropic causes and excellence in Town Government.

Palm Beach is alive and well – forever young because of the people who live, work and visit. Their presence throughout Palm Beach history has produced a special magic that makes the town unlike any other.

One simply has to enjoy and be grateful that history has been so good to the Town of Palm Beach-and to the people who made it what it is today. They are responsible for this book becoming a reality and we pay tribute to them within these pages:

Palm Beach, a Community Tribute.

Gail L. Coniglio

After 100 Years

After 100 Years

After over 100 years of graceful evolution, Palm Beach today is a fully developed community, world-renowned for its beauty, quality of life and small-town character. It is home to many of the world-famous. Approximately 9,000 citizens make Palm Beach their year-round home, with 20,000 more enjoying their seasonal residency during the winter months. All enjoy a wide variety of sports and activities during the 'season', notable for its multitude of charitable events benefiting a variety of worthy causes.

The Town is governed by an elected Mayor and a five-member Council and operates under the Council-Manager form of government, which provides a full range of municipal services. It has an active historic preservation program, comprehensive zoning standards and highly recognized public safety services and public works. Three miles of public beaches and a wide array of recreation programs, including award winning golf and tennis facilities, along with municipal docks, make Palm Beach a true paradise.

Town of Palm

Elected Officials

Gail L. Coniglio, Mayor

Robert N. Wildrick
Town Council President

William J. Diamond
Town Council President Pro Tem

Richard M. Kleid
Councilmember

Michael J. Pucillo
Councilmember

Penelope D. Townsend
Councilmember

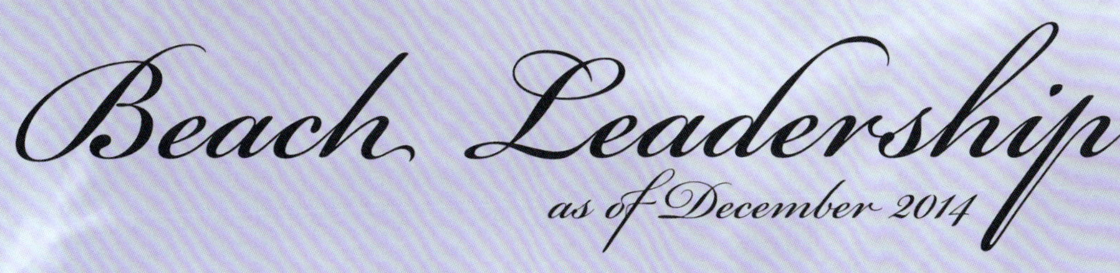

Beach Leadership
as of December 2014

Management Team

Peter B. Elwell
Town Manager

Thomas G. Bradford
Deputy Town Manager

Kirk Blouin
Director of Public Safety

Jay Boodheshwar, *Director of Recreation & Special Projects*

H. Paul Brazil
Director of Public Works

Danielle Olson
Director of Human Resources

John Page, *Director of Planning, Zoning & Building*

Jane Struder
Director of Finance

Playing in Paradise

Palm Beach began as a resort town and its population is still dominated by historical 'seasons'. It is located on a 14 mile barrier island on the east coast of Florida, with a year round population of approximately 9,000 residents. Every winter season (when the climate is more temperate) the town of Palm Beach swells to about 20,000, with hundreds of larger-than-life personalities returning to their winter residences to enjoy the weather and the outdoor freedom that it allows for avid golfers, tennis players, cyclists, nature lovers... and of course there are the pristine beaches.

"It's Time to Play!"... ***Palm Beach Recreation Center***

Power and sailboats have been moored at the town docks since the 1940s. Located in Lakeside Park between Peruvian and Brazilian Avenues, the docks have enjoyed a convenient location with ready access to the Palm Beach Inlet and Atlantic Ocean in addition to smooth sailing up and down the Intracoastal Waterway.

PHOTO CREDIT: Town of Palm Beach

Playing in Paradise
in the Town of Palm Beach

Photo: State Archives of Florida, Florida Memory, http://floridamemory.com
FM # 28216

Photo: State Archives of [illegible] Memory, http:
FM # 73494

Photo: State Archives of Florida, Florida Memory, http://floridamemory.com/items/show/160511, Detroit Publishing Co.

...emory.com

Photo: State Archives of Florida, Florida Memory, http://floridamemory.com
FM # 155748 Milliar, William N.

On the Beach

Palm Beach is located on a 14 mile barrier island located on the east coast of Florida, (called the "Gold Coast" for the wealth of its residents) with pristine beaches enjoyed by resident and tourist alike for more than 100 years.

Playing in Paradise...

Tennis at the Hotel Royal Poinciana

"Opened in February 1894 by Standard Oil tycoon and hotel and railroad empire builder Henry M. Flagler, the Colonial-style Hotel Royal Poinciana overlooking Lake Worth immediately put Palm Beach on the society map as the de-riguer winter destination of the Gilded Age, offering seasonal guests pastimes ranging from golf, tennis and strolls along the lake, to tea in it's famous Cocoanut Grove." *Courtesy of Palm Beach Daily News*

Phipps Ocean Park Tennis Center

2002 - The Phipps Ocean Park Tennis Center opened in February 2002 and features six Hydrogrid Hartru tennis courts with shade shelters. The center also features a pro shop and a decorative gated entrance plaza with a player/spectator pavilion. The courts are available seven days a week. Programs at the facility include drop-in play, doubles mixers, private lessons, clinics, league play, and a variety of special events. The center was awarded the Outstanding Tennis Facility Award by the USTA in 2003.

The Legacy of Golf...

PHOTO CREDIT: Nile Young, Jr.

The Breakers Palm Beach entices golfers with Florida's finest mix of vintage and contemporary golf experiences.

Enjoyed by celebrity, royalty and professional golfers alike through its first 100 Years, the Ocean Course provides an extraordinary vintage golf experience and a stunning golf and tennis clubhouse designed in the grand, 'Old Florida' style of architecture.

The course was originally laid out in 1896 by Alexander H. Findlay, who was hired by Flagler himself, and completely redesigned by famed golf course architect Brian Silva in 2000. Silva restored the vintage design characteristics of the state's oldest 18-hole course by addressing tee elevation and size, surface slopes, pin placement areas, and the integration of sand and grass-faced bunkers. The Ocean Course features elements such as random bunkering throughout the landscape (as opposed to a more modern, repetitive scheme) and fairways that weave between sandy hazards embodying an old-world sensibility.

Its contemporary counterpart is The Breakers Rees Jones® Course at Breakers West, located 11 miles west of the hotel. This course experienced a dramatic reconstruction in 2004, under the direction of its namesake, one of the golf industry's most renowned architects and future Golf Hall of Famer. The magnificent layout reflects Jones' incomparable neo-classic style and earned Golf Inc's 'Renovation of the Year' award. Together, these championship courses position the oceanfront resort as a great golf destination. Tim Collins, director of golf at the Ocean Course, explains, "The Breakers appeals to both avid golfers and those travelers who simply enjoy golfing while on vacation."

began at The Breakers

courtesy of The Breakers Palm Beach

PHOTO CREDIT: Bob Davidoff

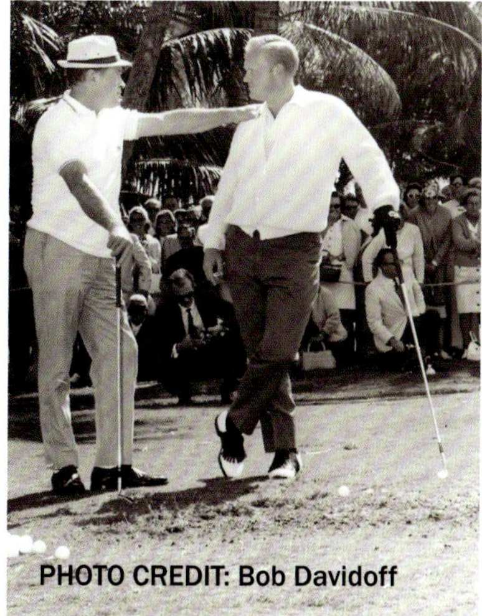

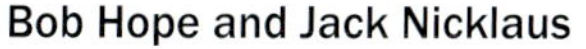

Bob Hope and Jack Nicklaus

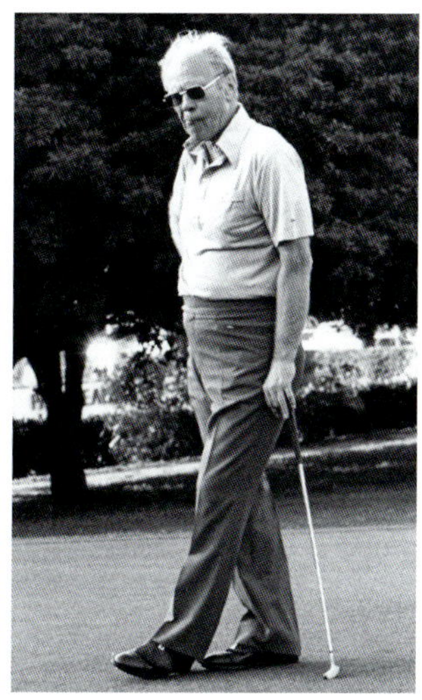

President Gerald Ford

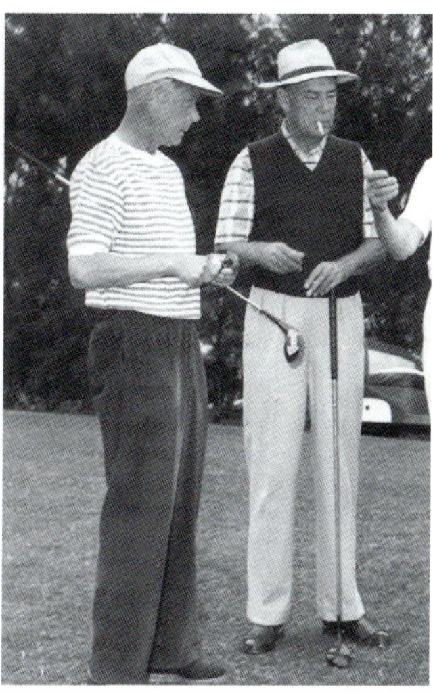

l-r: Duke of Windsor and Doc Holden, 1953

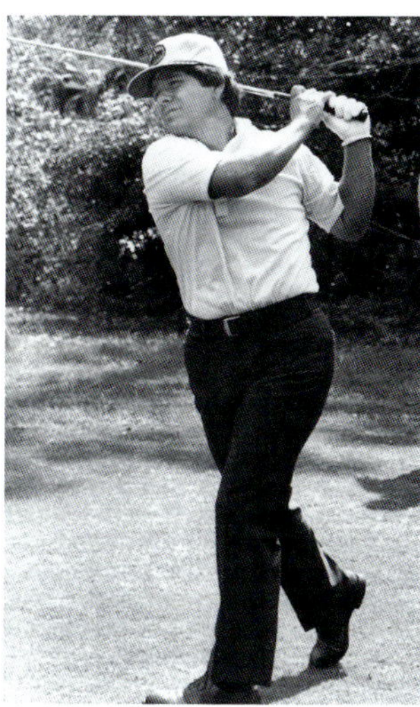

Lee Trevino

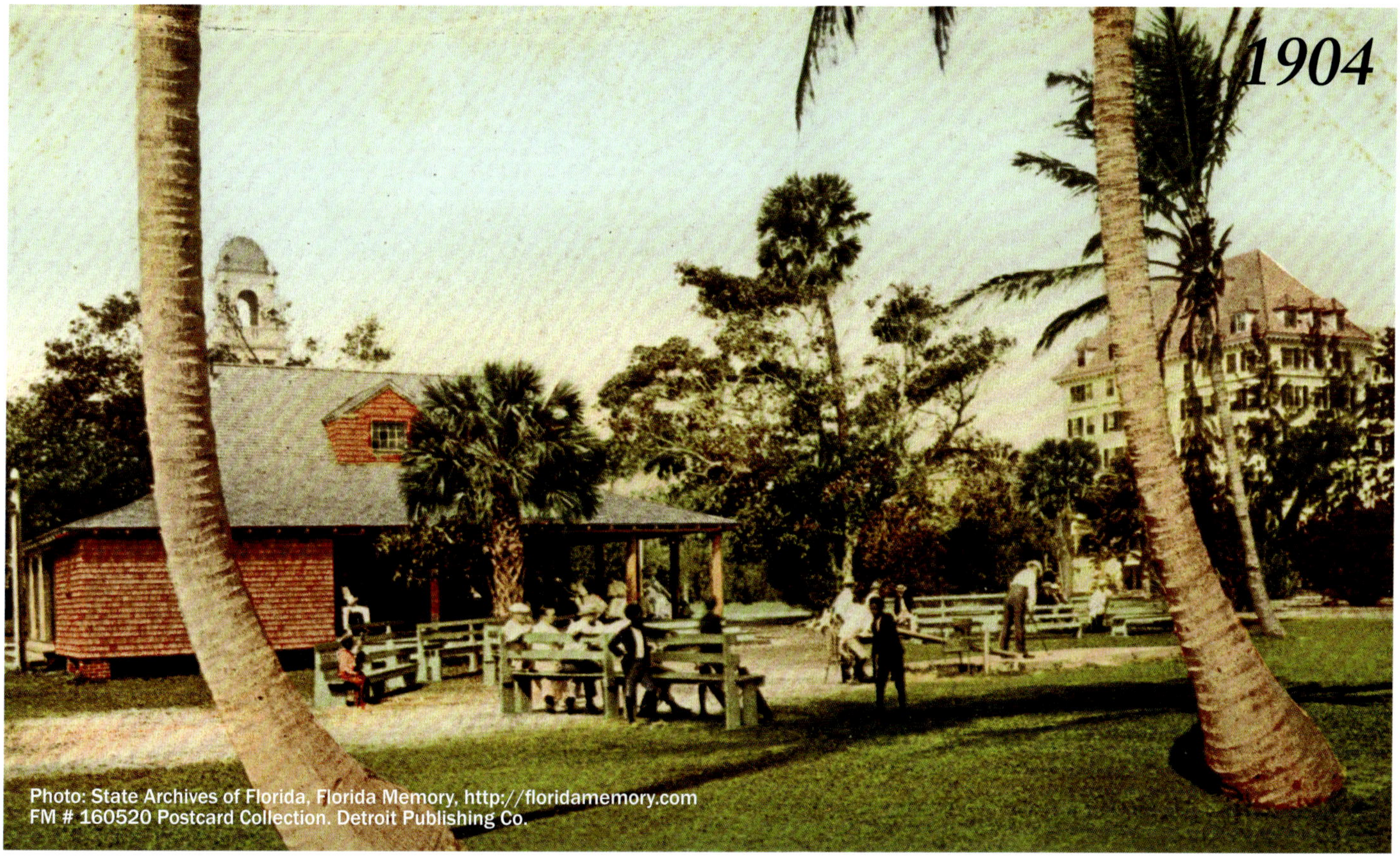

1904

Photo: State Archives of Florida, Florida Memory, http://floridamemory.com
FM # 160520 Postcard Collection. Detroit Publishing Co.

The Par-3 Golf Course

PHOTO CREDIT: Town of Palm Beach

Originally designed and privately owned from 1961 until 1973, the Palm Beach Par 3 Golf Course has a unique position between the Atlantic and the Intracoastal Waterway. The town purchased the course in 1973. Hall of Fame Golfer, Raymond Floyd, was instrumental in planning out the course's renovation and redesign, as well as the private fundraising efforts to complete the work. Re-opened in December 2009, the golf course has its new oceanside clubhouse which is open for breakfast, lunch and dinner.

The Par 3 Foundation, comprised of leading members of the Palm Beach community, raised the majority of the funds necessary to showcase this exceptional golf course. The foundation's inspiration was Maria Floyd, a tireless volunteer who believed deeply in the importance of the course for the town. It was she who was the driving force behind the clubhouse project; sadly, her death in 2012 denied her the opportunity to see her extraordinary work to completion, but her vision will live on with the new clubhouse.

Through the leadership of the Floyds, the Par 3 Foundation was created to collect funds for the completion of the course and its clubhouse. For those who know Floyd it should come as no surprise that this course, along with the many others he designed, focuses first and foremost on the player's experience. Skill, strategy and knowledge go into every Floyd-design course. Combining the art of architecture with the traditional philosophies of golf through the ages, the Par 3 exemplifies the course's place in the history of the town. It is said of Floyd that his grasp of integrity, intensity and excellence are reflected in all of his designs.

The Recreation Center

The Playground

The Palm Beach Recreation Center, 340 Seaview Avenue

In 1932, the Town of Palm Beach first established a Playground Committee to oversee and advise on public recreation facilities and programs. Appointed by the town council, this committee is now called the Recreation Advisory Commission. Due to the comprehensive thinking of the original group, a strong foundation for municipal recreational services was laid for all to enjoy. In 1975 a formal program was initiated with professional staff.

By 1982 the community recognized the need for modern facilities to answer the needs of a growing population. Monies for the facilities were raised by the 1982 and 1984 staging of the Palm Beach Follies. Singing, dancing, drama and tom-foolery brought Palm Beach locals – and some very famous personalities – to the stage to raise funds for the center, its tennis courts, playground and fields.

Today, the center oversees tennis at two locations, after-school programs and holiday camps. Sports and educational programs are available for children and adults.

Little Known....

Photo: State Archives of Florida, Florida Memory, http://floridamemory.com
FM # N036620

Lady in white reclining on the beach - Palm Beach, Florida

There was a patrolling 'beach censor' by the name of Connie Lewis. Her duty was to ask people revealing a little too much skin to leave the beach.

The Bathing Hour, Palm Beach, Fla.

206,561 J.V.

Photo: State Archives of Florida, Florida Memory, http://floridamemory.com

Photographers

Modern day scribes of Palm Beach…documenting the past and present – for future generations to remember. **Troy Devine**

The Photographer's Photographer

Mort Kaye

1916-2013

An indefatigable worker, Mort was well into his 90s when he formally 'retired' from the profession he loved, passing on his legacy to son Corby. Mort Kaye died at the age of 97.

As guardian of his father's cameras, Corby Kaye is carrying on Mort's legacy with the same understated style that puts people at ease and helps to capture the real personality and character. With a curious mind, having studied anthropology, coupled with the artistic talents provided by his parents, Corby Kaye has established his career based on his exceptional talents and grounded in the trust people have in the company's reputation.

As a New York native, Mort Kaye began photographing Palm Beach society in the 1940s and in the early 1950s became a Palm Beach resident. Known throughout town as 'the portrait photographer', Mort was able to capture the essence of the individual's personality and character with patience and humor. With camera in hand, he visited numerous social events throughout the season, marking historic events and notables.

The late Bob Davidoff and the late Lucien Capehart began their Palm Beach photographic careers under Mort Kaye's tutelage.

Forever the teacher, Mort referred to himself as the "Dean of Photographers" This is embodied in his instructions within the photo caption (below), referencing the photo (top right) of Prince Charles and Princess Diana (The Prince and Princess of Wales).

In case the subject comes up: photographing royalty isn't easy. At this 1986 dinner/ fundraiser at the Breakers, Prince Charles lent his name to the United World College Fund. To photograph the Prince and Princess, one could not speak to the royal couple unless spoken to; get no closer than 15 feet; could not change location after they arrived; and not stare at his ears. The Breakers went all out for the royal couple and uniformed elevator operators were on duty for the duration of the stay, and a special room was redecorated in case Charles or Diana needed to use a lavatory during the festivities. They were not so moved. As Prince Albert once commented: "You can never tell when you'll be called on to review the troops."

Photographs by Mort Kaye

Internationally acclaimed pianist and performer, Liberace with Mort Kaye

President George H. W. Bush and Mort Kaye

Actor Bob Hope at The Breakers Palm Beach with Mort Kaye

Princess Diana and Prince Charles of Wales, at The Breakers Palm Beach

President John F. Kennedy

Yoko Ono and John Lennon at The Colony Hotel

British Prime Minister Margaret Thatcher with Mort Kaye

First Lady Jaqueline Bouvier Kennedy

Living the Palm Beach Lifestyle

Robert Davidoff

1926-2004

The Town of Palm Beach's history can best be told by the photographers who captured the moments in pictures and recollections. Bob Davidoff began his island career in 1955 and went on to bring smiles to countless residents, visitors and celebrities. Best known for his longstanding relationship with the Kennedy family, Davidoff recorded the life stories of other Palm Beach residents like the Azqueta and Fanjul families. From rock stars, to royalty and the silver screen, Davidoff Studios captured an extraordinary time in Palm Beach's history. Rod Stewart, Michael Jackson, Andy Warhol, Phyllis Diller, Martha Stewart and Joan Rivers smiled broadly for Bob. Dukes and duchesses appeared, along with Prince Charles and Lady Diana, Princess Yasmin Aga Kan, Prince Andrew and heads of state such as Presidents George H.W. Bush, Gerald Ford and Ronald Reagan. Stars of the silver screen included Jack Benny, Bing Crosby, Ray Milland, Robin Williams and Debbie Reynolds kept the magic of the movies alive in paradise.

Robert Davidoff's sons have followed in their father's footsteps, continuing the tradition of preserving memories from today for many tomorrows. Michael, Ken and Daryl inherited the art of photography from their father in their teens and assisted on projects at an early age. Daryl still works with his mother Babe in the studio and together they continue the Palm Beach expectation of photographic perfection.

President John F. Kennedy with First Lady, Jaqueline Bouvier Kennedy and their children *John John* and Caroline outside their Palm Beach Home en route to Sunday Mass.

"I did not start working with Bobby until all the children were in school. Up until that time, he would come home every night and tell us about all the wonderful people he had met. People who lived in Palm Beach, celebrities, presidents, actors, actresses, etc. if he saw a show, he would come home at night and do the whole show for me. He should have been on the stage, he was a real ham. There are so many stories, there is not enough time or paper…Needless to say we have had a wonderful life in Palm Beach and have made so many friends, too numerous to mention but Bobby loved them all, and they loved him… and so do I". – Babe Davidoff

Photographs by Robert Davidoff

l-r: Chris Holmes, Greg Dodge Moran and Arlene Dahl

l-r: Fernando Lamas, Esther Williams and Bob Davidoff

Marlon Brando, 1955 with Brian Englund in the stroller, his brother Adam on the right. Kenny Davidoff far left, Michael Davidoff with teddy bear at the family home on Seminole Avenue.

George Hamilton and Susan Kohner

Bob Davidoff sets up his cameras in front of the Frank J. Hale's Royal Poinciana Playhouse

l-r: Davidoff family:
Daryl, Michael, Bob, Babe and Ken Davidoff

The Duke and Duchess of Windsor

Mrs. Marjorie Merriweather Post and J.Y. Arnold

Former first Lady Jaqueline Bouvier Kennedy Onassis with Bob Davidoff

Remembering a Legend

Lucien Capehart

1946-2012

Lucien's heart was captured by the area over forty years ago when he came on holiday and remained, capturing in turn the hearts and minds of a community. No subject escaped his careful, playful eye, his ability to capture the essence of his subject, with style and wit and an endearing manner of thoughtfulness and memory.

Lucien's ability to capture the nuance, the shadows, the mystery of place distinguished his work and his reputation as the go-to photographer. His easy-going disposition put everyone at ease; he could cajole as well as examine his subject's moods.

He would appear in photos now and again, but never as the focal point – his grace and demeanor filled the frame nonetheless. He was likable – he made others feel comfortable and he nurtured friendships over the years.

Commercial photography was another of Lucien's production. He knew how to sell a room, a feel, a mood and captured the designer's philosophy of style while preserving the integrity of the shot.

Events and Lucien were synonymous with success: the much sought after photographer of social and charitable events large and small did not need a PEEP list to know what and who needed to be covered. Ever gracious, even to those who might impose themselves into a shot, no one ever felt left out of the scene.

Weddings were a very special time for Lucien and the cast of friends and family members at the affair. The bride felt comfortable in his presence; the groom was able to laugh; the mother of the bride could relax, all knowing that Lucien had the situation well in hand and would capture the magic of the moment for years to come.

"Lucien taught me the art of capturing a moment. My staff and I will continue on his legacy for years to come and I am honored that he believed in me to carry on his artful tradition." - ***Carrie Bradburn***

Doctor, lawyer, philanthropist, doyen – their strength of character and personality became better known thanks to Lucien's kind and gentle ways. This unique ability to bring the person through the camera comes to very few. For those who had the privilege to have their portraits done by Lucien, the world benefited by the rare glimpse of humanity he brought to each image.

Lucien's death in February 2012 marked the end of a stellar photographic career that captured the style and essence of Palm Beach. His enthusiastic endorsement of the project will be missed, but his spirit and business vision will be carried on by Carrie Bradburn.

Lucien Capehart's spirit emanates – distinguished his life, defined his work and secured his legacy in the community.

With years of history behind him and a reputation that is nationally renowned, Lucien Capehart's hand chosen staff continue his vision for excellence, unparalleled quality and unequaled service.

"The perfect photograph happens in all of a split second. I have always subscribed to the theory that if a client is indeed confident enough to allow me to capture that second for them, that only the best I have given will ever do."
Lucien Capehart (1946-2012)

REMEMBERING.....

Troy Devine

1980-2013

PHOTO CREDIT: Lucien Capehart

Troy and Olympia

By Laurel Baker

Troy Alexander Devine was born November 17, 1980 in Toronto, Canada to Olympia Devine and the late Ralph Lawrence Devine, former Consul General for Liberia in Canada. Troy spent his early years roaming his maternal grandmother's conservation game farm in South Africa. It was the spirit of South Africa that inspired him and where his love of animals and his innate creative genius took root. His fearless enthusiasm and wonder enriched his childhood and created a treasure trove of talents in adulthood.

Arriving in the States in 1990, Troy and his mother settled in Palm Beach where he attended Palm Beach Day School and St. Clare Catholic School and was graduated from The Benjamin School. Troy furthered his education at Florida Atlantic University and the University of Central Florida. A world-view and his continued fascination with all things led Troy to positions in marketing, photography and business development at the Fairmont Chateau Lake Louise in Alberta, Van Style Inc. in Vancouver and the Royal Caribbean in Venice, Italy.

Having explored the world and encountering people from all walks of life, Troy became keenly aware of the disparities in society. This sensitivity to the unmet needs of many brought a new core focus on philanthropic initiatives to Devine Style, Inc., his mother's marketing, public relations and event-planning firm. Troy's arrival at the firm brought a new dimension to the company, with a strong ability to concentrate on fundraising for non-profits. His innate enthusiasm, creativity and drive broadened the scope of services to non-profit organizations. To

"Troy's leadership, work ethic, professionalism, and calmness during the hectic two months leading up to Palm Beach's Centennial weekend of celebrations was most impressive. There was no way we could have experienced the success we did without Troy (and Olympia) agreeing to take on this tremendous challenge. The wonderful memories created on April 15, 16, and 17, 2011, are a tribute to Troy and his legacy will live on in those memories. I will always cherish my time with Troy and the wonderful experiences we had during Palm Beach's Centennial. Every time I think about him, I smile."

— JAY BOODHESHWAR, TOWN OF PALM BEACH

name a few: MD Anderson Cancer Center; Habitat for Humanity, Peggy Adams Animal Rescue League; the Boys and Girls Club and many more benefitted from Troy's hard work.

The philanthropic enthusiasms he brought to his jobs were transferred to his invaluable contributions at Devine Style Inc. He partnered with his mother to stage such fundraising events as Palm Beach Fashion Week, Palm Beach Style Rocks, Windows of Worth, W Magazine special events, Mar-a-Lago Club fashion events… and most thrillingly, the very successful three day 2011 Palm Beach Centennial Celebration. The Palm Beach Centennial was managed by Troy with efficiency, humor and perspective along with Bill Bone, Centennial Chairman, Jay Boodheshwar, Town Director of Recreation and the council-appointed Palm Beach Centennial Commission. His unique talents and sheer will to accomplish a once-in-a-century event, in less than two months was unmatched… Troy's ability to coordinate time-lines, hundreds of volunteers, media deadlines and finances was masterful – and beyond successful, creating memorable events and happy participants who, to this day, speak in wonder that such a young man could do so much.

Troy was a gentle spirit of the world. Traveling near and far for business and pleasure, throughout his life he maintained the wide-eyed wonder of a child, relishing every person and place he encountered. Ever optimistic, patient, open and accepting, standing 6'4" head-and-shoulders above a crowd (in more ways than one) —Troy walked a very special road with wisdom and kindness.

"They say that trust is something that needs to be earned; but what if you could just look at a person and know that you can trust them with your life? It's an energy, it's in their eyes, their smile, their voice. It's something that can't be learned, it can't be faked; few have it, and most — do not.
An amazing heart, mind and soul are so hard to find in this crazy world and when you find it, you want to hold on to it with everything you have — Troy, a true friend. Not one of those that comes and goes, but one of those that comes and goes too soon."

— WENDY CARROLL

Troy Devine died peacefully of cardiac arrest on December 14, 2013 surrounded by close family. He is survived by his mother, Olympia Devine and his beloved Labrador, Chanel.

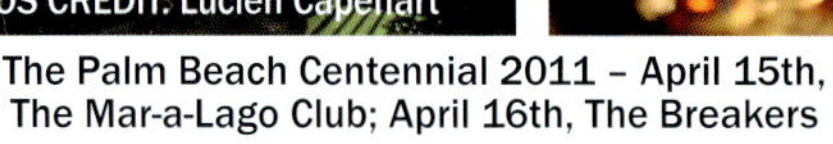
PHOTOS CREDIT: Lucien Capehart

The Palm Beach Centennial 2011 – April 15th, The Mar-a-Lago Club; April 16th, The Breakers

PHOTO CREDIT: Flagler Museum

April 17th, The Flagler Museum

Little Known....

PHOTO CREDIT: Mort Kaye

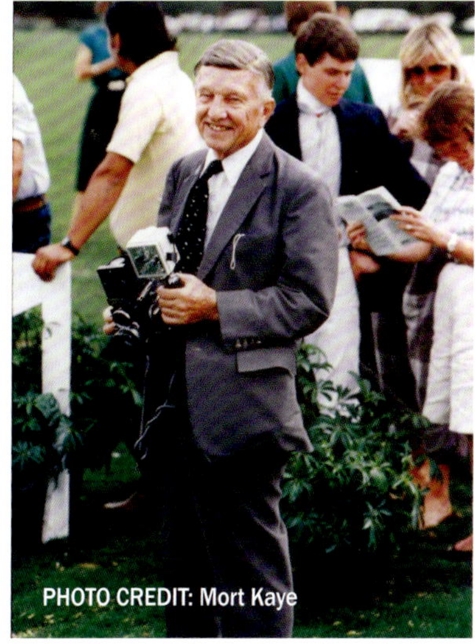

Bert Morgan (1904-1986) was a British born photographer who became well-known in the 1930's as a high society photographer - travelling between New York and Palm Beach. Together with his son, Richard they covered the Palm Beach social "season" in the 1950s.

Bert's photographs can be viewed on the walls of the Paramount Theatre. He inspired photographer Mort Kaye to become a society photographer in Palm Beach. This is confirmed by Mort Kaye's son Corby, who now carries the society photographer torch... and the rest (as they say) is history.

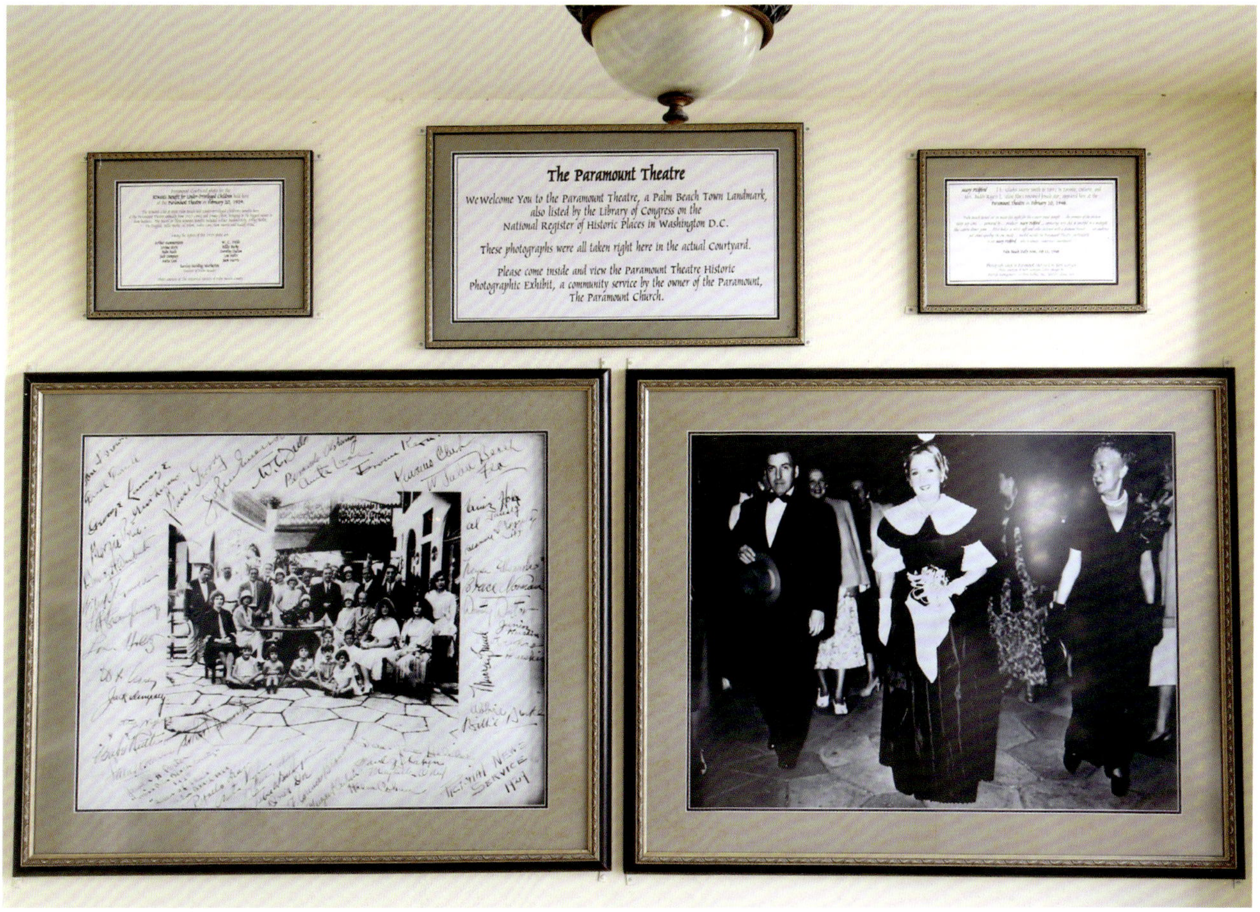

Bert Morgan's photographs (along with other photographer greats) can be seen on the walls of the Paramount Theatre.

Mary Pickford with Gladys Marie Smith in 1892 and Mrs. Buddy Rogers, silent films renowned female star appeared here at the Paramount Theatre on February 10, 1948.

Community Notables

This book was inspired by the many people profiled: their commitment to community and to the greater good are showcased here to inspire others. They have used their time and talents wisely. They have been generous in giving. Our community is all the better for their engagement and sharing of their many blessings. **Laurel Baker**

PHOTO CREDIT: Bob Davidoff

Helen Cluett

Born in China to parents who served as missionaries, Helen Cluett came to Palm Beach in 1959. Her commitment to family, church and community has distinguished her as a leader and role model to generations of Palm Beachers.

She has been recognized locally and nationally for her support of Republican issues and candidates, though always counseling voters to look at the character of the candidate, not the party affiliation.

Her board and event chair services to non-profits including Opportunity, Inc., the Episcopal Church of Bethesda-by-the-Sea, the Palm Beach Chamber, the Fellowship of Christians and Jews and the Historical Society set a standard for excellence, a knowledgeable leader with passion and compassion for the needs of others.

Her life and times in Palm Beach are a testament to the character of a town she loved very dearly.

Fitz Eugene Dixon, Jr. and Edith 'Edi' Dixon

A mighty powerhouse of ideas and execution, Fitz Dixon's good counsel led to the growth and development of institutions here and in Pennsylvania. He cared deeply about the heritage of place and demonstrated extraordinary leadership in the arts, religion, education and healthcare. The disciplines learned through his interest in sports greatly benefited the Society of the Four Arts where he served as board president and for whom the new education center is named. The Episcopal Church of Bethesda-by-the-Sea enjoyed the fruits of his varied interests. Good Samaritan Hospital's board was the recipient of his sound judgments. Few in the community match the diversity of Dixon's interests and commitment to the guiding principles he believed in as teacher, benefactor and visionary.

Edi has led by example, directing her energies to systematic problem-solving and efficient actions. She has not merely carried on Fitz's legacy, but added a greater strength to the goals envisioned by institutions such as the Four Arts, a legacy that is a testament to her many talents.

PHOTO CREDIT: Courtesy of Palm Beach Daily News

PHOTO CREDIT: Courtesy of Palm Beach Daily News

Alexander W. Dreyfoos

Inventor, investor, philanthropist and much, more more. A true Renaissance Man for the ages, Dreyfoos has contributed to the tapestry of Palm Beach County in large part due to his interest and curiosity in so many areas.

Whether in electronics, broadcasting, the biosciences or culture, his vision has always been clear, his commitment unwavering. He was the force behind the creation of the Kravis as a performing arts center, the growth of the Dreyfoos School of the Arts, one of the premier magnet school in the country, the advancement of the sciences as the future industry in Palm Beach County with his involvement with the Scripps and Max Planck research institutions. The Cultural Council for the county was established by him – and has made the area the leading cultural center for the arts in the state.

Dreyfoos is an exceptional individual of diverse tastes and interests, filled with an enthusiasm for life and the heart to share with his community.

Dame Celia Lipton Farris

Born in England, Dame Farris captured the world's heart through the theatre. As Peter Pan, she rose to international prominence over the years with her singing, painting and humanitarian efforts. Hers was a commanding presence as one of the most photographed and photogenic entertainer, recording star and actress on television and in films.

There were few charities that did not benefit from her leadership and generosity over the years. Most notable among her philanthropic efforts were funds for the Victor Farris Pavilion at Good Samaritan Hospital, given to honor her late husband, Victor, a renowned inventor; the Kravis Center, the Foundation for the Preservation of the Great American Songbook and AIDS research. Her generosity continues through the Farris Foundation.

She was honored with the Clare Barton Award and the Gloria Swanson Humanitarian Award from the American Cinema Foundation.

PHOTO CREDIT: Bob Davidoff

The Fanjul Family

2nd row: seated l-r: Pepi and Emila Fanjul, Mrs. Norberto Azqueta, Mr. and Mrs. Alfonso Fanjul Sr., Maria Cristina (Tina) and Alfonso Fanjul
Back Row, 2nd from left is Norberto Azqueta with his two sons on either side of him
The rest are their children, nieces and nephews. 1979

For over a century, the Fanjul family has been identified with the sugar industry. In 1959, Castro's government seized their 400,000 acres of sugar cane. The family arrived in Florida and proceeded to do what they have done best: they secured land in western Palm Beach County and began planting again. Starting with 4000 acres, their holdings have grown substantially over the years.

The purchase of Gulf & Western Industries added more fields and diversified their operations. In addition to planting more sugar cane, they acquired Casa de Campo, a residential resort community in the Dominican Republic.

The emphasis on family ties is a mark of the successes realized over the past century and a half. The Fanjuls take pride in their history and the future they have built as leaders in the community. Their support of educational initiatives is the hallmark of the response to the pressing needs of others. Beyond the title 'First Family of Florida Sugar', the Fanjul family reflects the passion, compassion and support that is a matchless template for others to achieve.

PHOTO Courtesy of: Par 3 Golf Course

Maria and Ray Floyd

Through the leadership of the Floyds, the Par 3 Foundation was created to collect funds for the completion of the course and its clubhouse. For those who know Floyd it should come as no surprise that this course, along with the many others he designed, focuses first and foremost on the player's experience. Skill, strategy and knowledge go into every Floyd-design course. Combining the art of architecture with the traditional philosophies of golf through the ages, the Par 3 exemplifies the course's place in the history of the town. It is said of Floyd that his grasp of integrity, intensity and excellence are reflected in all of his designs.

Robert 'Bob' M. and Jane R. Grace

Individually and as a couple, Bob and Jane Grace are the standard bearers of true citizens. Their tireless efforts to preserve, protect and propagate all that is good about Palm Beach have touched every aspect of life on the island.

Leadership, through government service, the Society of the Four Arts, Preservation and animal rescue has enriched the community and served as an unparalleled example of selfless dedication. Buildings have been named to honor them – celebrations attended – goodly letters written; all pale in comparison to the lasting mark they have left on the character of Palm Beach.

PHOTO CREDIT: Courtesy of Palm Beach Daily News

PHOTO CREDIT: Mort Kay

George Hamilton and Ann Hamilton

That smile – that tan – that ever-cheerful attitude – how fortunate to have a 'townie' of such accomplishment and grace. Besides his varied acting career, George has shared his life story as an author. Son to Ann Hamilton, he and his brother drove across country with their mother, gathering memorable experiences along the way. However far their traveled, Palm Beach always beckoned and home they came to a warm welcome. Indeed, the boys were groomed for the public eye and public engagement, carrying on the Palm Beach tradition of community activism and pride of place.

Bobbi and Dr. Harry Horwich

Political activists, patrons of the arts, noted philanthropists, this dynamic duo has added to the tapestry of exceptional citizens in the Town of Palm Beach. Their wide-range of interests and commitment to causes ranging from environmental concerns, libraries, the League of Women Voters, beach re-nourishment and very special arts programs have distinguished them as community leaders with a passion for all that is right and good about Palm Beach.

PHOTO CREDIT: Lucien Capehart

PHOTO CREDIT: Courtesy of Palm Beach Daily News

Frances Archibold Hufty

Frances Hufty distinguished herself throughout life as a woman of vision and determination. These qualities have been shared by her family over three generations and have contributed greatly to the Town of Palm Beach and the nation.

She was an early proponent of environmental causes and conservation efforts. Two noteworthy endeavors include the Archibold Biological Station and the Pine Jog Environmental Education Center.

Ever gracious, with an eye to beauty, Frances Hufty's contributions have brought invaluable benefits to all. As her daughter, Page Lee Hufty noted during the centennial year, "We share an island graced by the legacy of inspired architects and amateur gardeners – a place where constantly surprising floral and bird life keep us tropical folks endlessly bewitched and amused.". Frances Archibold Hufty had an invaluable hand in this creation and preservation.

Mary and Philip Hulitar

The Hulitars were an exceptional couple as leaders in Palm Beach. Blending the talents of a prominent American couturier with a public-spirited individual, Philip and Mary Hulitar contributed an unmatched focus on beauty.

The sculpture gardens at the Society of the Fours Arts are a tribute to Philip's artistic talents as well as their mutual appreciation of Palm Beach. Completed in 1980, the gardens are a timeless gift to the community. They stand as examples of visionary leadership.

PHOTO CREDIT: Bob Davidoff

Howard and Michele Kessler

PHOTO CREDIT: Lucien Capehart

Michele and Howard Kessler have shared their significant involvement with the medical community in a host of engagements with nationally-recognized institutions such as Brigham and Women's Hospital, the Dana Farber Cancer Institute, Massachusetts General Hospital's Council for Psychiatry and Global Ambassadors of the Measles Initiative for the American Red Cross. Their leadership skills and vision, coupled with their philanthropic service, have greatly impacted many around the world.

Howard Kessler pioneered the concept of the affinity credit card with MBNA in 1982 and remains a leading entrepreneur for financial services firms around the world. He has been recognized by numerous charitable institutions for his countless achievements across the country.

Michele Kessler serves as Director of Community Relations at The Kessler Group and co-founder and director of the Kessler Family Foundation. She serves on the boards of the William J. Clinton Foundation, the American Ireland Fund, the Foundation for Art and Preservation in Embassies, the Ayenda Foundation and the Global Health Advisor Council at Harvard Medical School.

Together, Michele and Howard Kessler have brought their leadership skills and inspiration to the Town of Palm Beach, actively supporting, by word and deed, the Town of Palm Beach United Way, Palm Beach Civic Association, the Preservation Foundation, American Cancer Society and other agencies that directly impact the health and welfare of the community.

At home in Palm Beach, The Kennedy Shriver family

Back Row l-r: Sargent Shriver, Maria Shriver, Eunice Kennedy Shriver, Anthony Shriver, Linda and Mark Shriver, Jeanine (Mark's wife). *Front Row l-r:* Alina Shriver (Anthony's wife) and children.
Courtesy of the Kennedy Home, Palm Beach

PHOTO CREDIT: Bob Davidoff

President John F. Kennedy with First Lady, Jaqueline Bouvier Kennedy and their children *John John* and Caroline outside their Palm Beach Home en route to Sunday Mass

The Kennedy Family

1933 - Joseph P. Kennedy Sr. bought oceanfront property as a family vacation home which later became known as President John F. Kennedy's "Winter White House." This is where the family patriarch taught the nation's future leaders to swim, and where young President John F. Kennedy chose his Cabinet.

The house became an historic landmark and was purchased by New York banker, John K. Castle. It came with most of its original furnishings and restored by its new owner – as an historical legacy.

PHOTO: State Archives of Florida, Florida Memory, http://floridamemory.com
FM # 79619 Dept. of Commerce Collection

1961-1963: President Kennedy's "Winter White House" was his family's Palm Beach estate

PHOTO CREDIT: Lucien Capehart

David and Julia Koch

As leaders in the philanthropic communities of New York and Palm Beach, the Kochs represent the quintessential picture of leadership, commitment and family values. David's work ethic has been recognized for the countless hours of successful leadership in the oil industry. His is the approachable personality, filled with glee and particularly passionate when it comes to his family.

David Koch has demonstrated that he stands behind his beliefs and supports causes near to his heart. His philanthropic activities have touched upon all areas of society, including medical health, science, theatre, art and education.

As part of his sense of community, and in recognition of his philanthropy, Mr. Koch acted as an Event Chair for the All Town Centennial Palm Beach Celebration 2011. The centennial celebrations became a true family affair with the Koch brothers serving as hosts (David and Bill Koch).

Julia has distinguished herself as the fresh face of major fundraising efforts focused on the arts. Her quiet demeanor and focus extend as well to the nurturing of home life and the happiness enjoyed in the Koch household.

A strong woman stands behind this exceptional individual. Julia Koch stands tall as a wife, mother and model of community involvement. Her stellar career working with Adolfo during the Reagan administration provided her with the style and grace to chair the Metropolitan Museum of Art's annual Costume Institute gala which paid tribute to the late Gianni Versace.

They epitomize the style and elegance that befits Palm Beach while serving as exemplars of good citizens.

William 'Bill' Koch and Bridget Rooney Koch

William 'Bill' Koch – founder and Chief Executive Office of Oxbow Carbon LLC. Ranked as one of the 25 most generous individuals in the United States by The Journal of Philanthropy in 2011, Mr. Koch may be best-remembered for his mission to help less fortunate children receive a quality education.

Mr. Koch's dream began as a child when he learned that a local Quanah businessman had financed his father's college education at MIT. Over the years, Mr. Koch has contributed money, time and energy to help individuals, teachers and classrooms get the needed support. He has donated musical instruments and tutoring help to disadvantaged children in Palm Beach County; computers and software for children with learning disabilities, and funds for science programs around the world. For students with a keen interest in art, the Kochs regularly open their home to hundreds of students annually. Access to one of the country's finest private art collections is a priceless opportunity to future artists, collectors and patrons.

Oxbridge Academy, a private high school in West Palm Beach, was founded by Mr. Koch. With a donation of $60 million, one of Koch's greatest satisfaction was seeing the doors open in 2011. Nearly 80 percent of the students at Oxbridge receive some form of financial assistance. One of the key components to the school's outstanding curriculum is to be found in the faculty – individuals whose enthusiasm for learning have made this new institution a remarkable addition to the community at large.

Bill Koch and his wife Bridget Rooney Koch reside in Palm Beach, Florida, along with their six children. As part of his sense of community, and in recognition of his philanthropy, Mr. Koch acted as an Event Chair for the All Town Centennial Palm Beach Celebration 2011.

The centennial celebrations became a true family affair with the Koch brothers serving as hosts (Bill and David Koch). Bill's eclectic interests in all things, Wild West, sailing, engineering, wine and family brought an added joy to the event. Bridget Rooney Koch served as an outstanding ambassador. Her family background in sports and politics brought the necessary polish to this community affair.

PHOTO CREDIT: Barbara Vaugh

PHOTO CREDIT: Courtesy of Palm Beach Daily News

Terry Allen Kramer

The artistry and sheer 'wow' power of the centennial celebrations are as much a reflection of the supporting hosts. Her extensive background in finance and theatre is evidenced by the outstanding list of Broadway productions.

Engaging and enthusiastic, Ms. Kramer's leadership involvement and generous support of the Palm Beach Centennial was a classic extension of her interests and talents.

Estee Lauder

Never question what magic can happen in the kitchen. When Estee Lauder began her cosmetic empire in the 1940s, it happened in the kitchen. By 1946 the 'first lady of beauty' founded the family-owned empire.

The brand became an international favorite. Coupled with Estee's study of the psychology of packaging, women everywhere had at least one of the items from her growing product line. What is known of cosmetic marketing today has its roots at Estee Lauder – the packaging, color selections, gifts with purchase were pure Estee.

The Lauders arrival in Palm Beach created a new stir – invitations to their home were much sought after. Entertainment on South Ocean Boulevard brought together a stunning mix of people and personalities.

PHOTO CREDIT: Mort Kaye

Estee Lauder with her son Leonard A. Lauder

PHOTO CREDIT: Lucien Capehart

Paul and Kathy Leone

The consummate hotelier and leader of The Breakers Palm Beach, Paul Leone is one of the most engaging and engaged residents in Palm Beach. In addition to directing a staff of 2000 in an historic building, he serves by example.

Having received his accounting degree and working as a CPA, Paul transferred that attention to detail to every activity he participated in. Education, sports, United Way, chamber leadership and town service have all benefited by his leadership.

With his wife, Kathy, he has raised four sons - sharing his enthusiasm and respect for the living history that is The Breakers Palm Beach and its contributions to the development of one of the most special towns in the world.

Frayda and George Lindemann (not pictured)

Visionaries, indeed. From the sale of his family's eyecare company, George has had the uncanny ability to see the next trend, be it cable, mobile or energy.

Combine this talent with the exceptional leadership Freda has shown in the arts, most notably opera, and you have a winning team that shared their considerable insights into support of the Palm Beach Centennial.

PHOTO CREDIT: Courtesy of Palm Beach Daily News

PHOTO CREDIT: Mort Kaye

David and Hildegard 'Hillie' Mahoney

Long considered one of the leading power couples in Palm Beach, they were often described as exemplary representatives of all that is good and sound about the town. Interested in a wide variety of issues and causes, the Mahoneys are considered leaders in the field of neurological sciences. Their early involvement and support of brain and behavior research distinguishes them in the town. Such broad-reaching engagement on an international level is a testimony to the Mahoney's extraordinary contributions to raise the bar on charitable giving.

Important behavioral studies to discover the link between the molecular workings of the brain cells and human cognition will benefit all of mankind. Their vision far exceeds the imagination. Their commitment unmatched. With funds supporting studies at Harvard and Columbia, the world is being led by the far-reaching hopes for a better world.

The Matthews Family

As an heir to the Flagler legacy on Palm Beach, Will Matthews has carried on the traditions set by his ancestors through his involvement with the community. In addition to his services to the school, Palm Beach Day Academy, Eaglebrook School, the Four Arts and the Community Foundation, he plays an active role in the Kenan Flagler Business School at the University of North Carolina at Chapel Hill.

Jean's quiet grace and keen eye can be seen in her extraordinary photography. Recognized by the Garden Club of America, Jean's photos tell stories, inviting one in to explore as she has and capture the beauty. Her recent calendar of monthly Florida blooms has given locals a new appreciation for the seasons in Florida as well as an opportunity to explore the beauty of the island.

PHOTO CREDIT: Bob Davidoff

(l - r) Matthews Family: George Jr., Jeane F., Kelly, Betsy, George Sr. Front: Elizabeth

PHOTO CREDIT: Lucien Capehart

George and Betsy Matthews

Change has never been a stranger to the Matthews family, they were usually at the forefront. As Henry Flagler's great-grandson, George has carried on the family interests in real estate and commercial investments. George Matthews tireless efforts to realize his mother's pledge to restore Whitehall as an historic house museum were realized. Town service as a member of the town council for sixteen years, eight as council president, further testify to a man committed to family and community.

"What would Betsy do?" There is no finer tribute to honor the intelligence and wisdom of Betsy Matthews and her sense of justice and judgment. Numerous organizations have benefited from her good counsel and commitment.

As a couple, they have served as the exemplars of leadership, receiving local and national recognition by their peers. Whether a charity chairs or board presidents, the Matthews have brought charm, sophistication and a sense of community.

Mildred Brown 'Brownie' McLean

With an indomitable spirit and a smile that is brighter than the Hope Diamond, Mildred Brown 'Brownie' McLean is a national treasure. Indeed, who needed the Hope Diamond, actually owned by her in-laws, when you are Brownie?

Her enthusiasm is infectious, her interests and charitable endeavors have an international reach, including the Global Futures Foundation. Honored by numerous organizations for her tireless efforts on their behalf, including the American Red Cross.

PHOTO CREDIT: Bob Davidoff

Hermé de Wyman Miro

Born and educated in Austria, Mrs. Miro's artistic talents in music, dance and painting provided her with an entrée to international distinction. Through her travels and life-long experiences, she became acutely aware of the needs in society and set about to address them through the creation of the International Society in 1983. Together with her husband, Rene de Wyman, Hermé brought together an eclectic, fascinating group of individuals to share their cultures and their passion for the arts, education and health and welfare issues.

Her many contributions to the welfare of others has included the Palm Beach Opera, the Palm Beach Roundtable and countless other organizations, including President Eisenhower's Volunteer Action Center initiative in 1972 for which she and her husband received a White House Citation. Her fondness of butterflies, often adorning her hair, reflect the soring spirit of her imagination and commitment to making the world more beautiful through good deeds.

Dudley and Peggy Moore

PHOTO CREDIT: Lucien Capehart

When the Atlanta insurance mogul came to Palm Beach, he and his wife brought the joy of living to town along with a deep sense of pride and perfection. In addition to their southern charm and hospitality, they set about to making Palm Beach a better place by their sense of history and preservation efforts.

The creation of a garden to complement their carefully restored house set the Moores apart as the new standard of concerned, involved citizens committed to their community.

Their involvement with the Landmarks Commission and the Garden Club, the Four Arts and Preservation Foundation exemplify the best of what Palm Beach is all about.

Charles and Dorothy Munn

"Mr. Palm Beach" – a legendary figure of style and grace. Many have aspired to be like him, but none could match the sartorial splendor or sophistication that defined the Palm Beach era that he and his family epitomized. Others have assumed the title, only to be dismissed as pretenders.

He and his brother lived side by side on the ocean in fabulous houses named Amado and Louwana – names that invited gaiety and memorable celebrations of life. Theirs was an era that cannot be replicated, along with the people who lived it were originals of a gentlemanly past.

PHOTO CREDIT: Palm Beach Daily News

PHOTO CREDIT: Courtesy of the Historical Society of PBC

Amado-Munn Estate

PHOTO CREDIT: Mort Kaye

William and Alice Zimmer Pannill

The quiet elegance and graciousness of the Pannills brings back memories of old Palm Beach when life was simple, relaxed and unpretentious. Kit is well-known for her hospitality and encyclopedic knowledge of plants and flowers.

Bill, too, was world-renowned for his accomplishments in the garden, particularly with daffodils. As Palm Beach Centennial hosts, they epitomized the style and affability of the community they are proud to call home.

James and Susan Patterson

Despite his having had an illustrious career in advertising, and having published prior to his retirement in 1996, the reading public's love affair with James Patterson became quite passionate with the introduction of FBI agent Alex Cross. Since devoting himself fulltime to writing, Patterson publishes no fewer than two books a year. Character development, intrigue and action come together to create memorable adventures.

Many of these adventures have been made into movies – a testament to the writer knowing his reader. More importantly, Patterson has created a number of philanthropic programs to encourage reading, to train teachers and to support student scholarships. His enthusiasm for all things Palm Beach was evident in his generous support of the Palm Beach Centennial.

PHOTO CREDIT: Courtesy of Palm Beach Daily News

Patty Myura

Patty Myura has proven to be a dedicated Palm Beach community member, serving as an innovator and philanthropic fundraiser for many charities. In the process of being an agent of change, she has changed the lives and aspirations of many in Palm Beach County.

Patty's innovative spirit and entrepreneurial years - as a businesswoman and owner of a clothing store chain, formed the basis for many of the charity projects she helped develop. She has assisted many organizations from the ground up - helping them raise millions of dollars to achieve their mission goals. Borne into a philanthropic and entrepreneurial family, Patty inherited an ingrained moral code and work ethic, setting her destiny on a path to make a difference in the lives of others. Her mother installed in her the fact that helping others should be for all the right reasons... and done quietly.

Ever the visionary, her next venture led her to the casino gaming industry, a transformational business initiative that changed the profile of Atlantic City. And the city continued to grow through her presidency of the Atlantic City Chamber of Commerce, chairing the Governor's Conference in Atlantic City and honoring city leadership with Mayor's Day. Ad Executive Director of the Miss Atlantic City Pageant, she raised the standards of the show to professional production-based benchmarks other pageants would soon adopt.

Good neighbors and good deeds were matched when the Myuras lived on Brazilian Avenue and made the acquaintance of **Eleanor Patterson Reeves** who lived around the corner on Cocoanut Row. They shared an enthusiasm for charitable work and worked together for years. Having served by example, Mrs. Reeves sought strong leadership and fiscal stewardship in the management of her foundation. The foundation's mission is strongly focused on children and their wellbeing.

Patty Myura was made head of the **Reeves Foundation** and set to work to identify those social service agencies in Palm Beach County that met the foundation's guidelines. Most notably, the Center for Family Services distinguished itself. It was Patty's intent to memorialize Ms. Reeves with a living/permanent program.

The Center of Family Services has become an integral community project. The Pat Reeves Village, a temporary housing facility provides local families with a "hands up" while developing the necessary skills and information they will need to be self-sufficient. Patty remains the force behind the Center, and continues to fulfill the Pat Reeves philanthropic legacy - together with the Foundation team donates to worthy causes for children. In addition to the Village, the Eleanor Patterson Reeves Foundation supports 25-30 local charities each year.

All good works deserve recognition and the communities Patty has served were grateful to award her such notable accolades as the 1982 Atlantic City Woman of the Year.

In 2012, she was awarded the Lifetime Achievement Award by the Center for Family Services as well as being recognized as the Outstanding Volunteer Fundraiser by the Association of Fundraising Professionals.

Read more about Patty Myura, The Center for Family Services and the Eleanor Patterson Reeves Foundation on page 210 of the Organization section.

> *"In the 23 years I have been in Palm Beach, I have had many experiences with many different and interesting people. To this day I am still excited to meet them. But, most of all I value the Palm Beach Giving Spirit – everyone gets together to have a good time at the numerous charity events. However, it's not just to enjoy a party with friends, it's all for a good cause."*

True to her affection for Palm Beach, Patty Myura occupies a classic Palm Beach home built in 1934 by renowned architect John Volk. John Charles Thomas, world-famous opera singer, commissioned Volk to construct the house for his mother. Thomas assisted in the Volk design by developing the proper acoustical sound flow for the house to properly accommodate his practice sessions while visiting Palm Beach.

Lois Pope

Lois Pope has received national acclaim for her unrelenting support of a diverse area of interests, ranging for medical research, recognition of disabled veterans, education, the arts and animal welfare. She has accomplished a great deal through her dedication to the foundations established to provide immediate funding to critical issues. Like the marathon runner she is, Lois sees no distractions as she sets sight on her goals.

Medical research, particularly neurological research on paralysis, has gained ground through the Lois Pope LIFE Center at the University of Miami and home to the Miami Project to Cure Paralysis.

In a like vein, Lois approached the forgotten soldiers left disabled and sought to recognize their valor through the LIFE Memorial in Washington, DC. This memorial serves to recognize the more than 3 million veterans.

Leaders in Furthering Education has provided disadvantaged and disabled children with camp experiences and scholarships for area students who have demonstrated the value of volunteering.

The performing arts have been the recipient of Lois's generosity, notably the Palm Beach Opera. The Armory Art Center's continuing growth in scheduling classes and exhibitions has greatly enriched the cultural base of the county. Public television has benefited from her service as well.

All creatures, great and small, have benefited from Lois's generosity, notably, The American Humane Association, where she sponsors the annual Hero Dog Awards in LA and donated two Lois Pope Red Star™ Rescue Vehicles. Her work locally with the Peggy Adams Animal Rescue League provided them with a new mobile pet adoption unit.

Such vision and generosity has been recognized around the world, acknowledging the singular strength of spirit that is Lois Pope. Honored by her peers in the fundraising arena as Philanthropist of the Year in 2008, she has been honored by the Miami Chamber of Commerce, was a recipient of the Ellis Island Medal of Honor and received honorary degrees from Chestnut Hill College and from the Rabbinical College of America.

Lois Pope was named a Daily Point of Light by President George H. W. Bush, a fitting recognition for the tireless leadership she has provided – and a shining example of all that is right and good.

Ashley and Ogden Phipps

The Phipps Family

With quiet grace and vision, the Phipps family created a legacy of commitment to community and family. Their generosity in providing land to Palm Beach and West Palm Beach for the perpetual enjoyment by many distinguishes their imprint on the future.

Development of parcels such as the Poinciana Plaza and later Phipps Estates demonstrated an understanding of changing times and adaptation while preserving the integrity of place. Their role in wealth management and the philanthropic needs of their Bessemer clients have continued the legacy of giving for the public good.

PHOTO CREDIT: Courtesy of Historical Society of Palm Beach County

Casa Beneitta - the Phipps Estate

PALM BEACH Young Society
The Magazine for Young Socialites
NOVEMBER 2013
American Red Cross
Beach Bash
honors Lilly Pulitzer
Saturday, December 28, 2013
THE BEACH CLUB

Lillian Pulitzer Rousseau

PHOTO CREDIT: Bob Davidoff

Born to a legendary family, Lilly Pulitzer Rousseau would become the first-name-only lady of fashion. Filled with joy and an eye for color, the Lilly phenomena took the world by storm, proving again that Palm Beach was the epicenter. Playful designs and brilliant colors combined to launch the "Palm Beach Look" – casual, slightly sassy and ever so practical: her first goal was to hid juice stains on her clothes while working at her Via Mizner juice stand. The rest is history.

Married at 19 to Peter Pulitzer, with whom she had three children, they later divorced. Family gathering continued in the great house she shared with her second husband, Enrique Rousseau. Lilly was a legend and an inspiration to all with whom she came in contact. Recognized by Palm Beach Atlantic University in 2008 as a Woman of Distinction, her impact on the community is filled with the same joyfulness as her whimsical designs.

James Ponce

Esteemed historian, James Ponce speaking at the Worth Avenue re-design ceremony - 2011

His charm has graced every legendary hotel on Palm Beach – and he continues his extraordinary retelling of The Breakers Palm Beach's history on weekly tours of the landmarked resort created by Henry Flagler. He even bears a striking resemblance to Flagler – along with a passion for everything that has made this island paradise so very special.

Born in St. Augustine, Florida, a descendent of the legendary Ponce de Leon, Jim has clearly found the Fountain of Youth as he continues to share the extraordinary stories of Palm Beach places and faces over the century, having recently turned 97-years old.

PHOTO CREDIT: Lucien Capehart

Tom Quick

His is the face and character of the new generation of philanthropists. Leading by example, Tom Quick's engagement with the community is a testament to his character.

A graduate of Fairfield University with a degree in business, Quick & Reilly/Fleet Street Securities grew under Tom's leadership as one of the nation's premier discount brokerage firms. 1998 marked Tom's retirement from the firm, but his greater engagement with community issues.

Wide ranging interests both nationally and locally brought Tom's talents and leadership skills to Cold Spring Harbor Laboratories, the National Corporate Theatre Fund, Inner-City Scholarship Foundation, the American Ireland Fund, Best Buddies, Hospice of Palm Beach, Dreher Park Zoo, and the Norton Museum of Art. Ever willing to contribute, his is the standard to which all should aspire.

David Reese

Of pioneer stock, David Reese carries on the spirit of adventure and leadership set by his family which settled on Palm Beach in 1876. This has been a family of firsts – with "Cap" Dimick, David's great-grandfather, serving as the town's first mayor, opened the first bank and is the first 'person' you see when crossing the middle bridge onto the island.

David's spirit of adventure includes his love of the ocean and surfing – what first drew the family to this barren island, before their modest hotel opened, continues to captivate David and his family: natural beauty, a communion with sun and surf and an abiding pride of place.

PHOTO CREDIT: Courtesy of Palm Beach Daily News

PHOTO CREDIT: Courtesy of Palm Beach Daily News

Janet Reynolds

The history of Palm Beach could not be complete without the inclusion of the Reynolds family and their countless contributions to the growth and development of the town.

With landmark memories seen in the First National Bank of Palm Beach building, Janet has continued in the remarkable heritage with her faithful involvement with the Rehabilitation Center for Children and Adults, along with the Norton Museum of Art, the Society of the Four Arts and those newer social service agencies addressing the growing needs of the wider community.

Earl E.T. Smith and Lesly Stockard Smith

Sophisticated, savvy and resilient, Lesly Smith possesses extraordinary gifts of leadership and humor. Wife to an ambassador, philanthropist and former town council member and mayor, Lesly's astute observations and natural curiosity have created a legacy for Palm Beach that few could match.

With a world-view, she has redefined the Palm Beach woman. While eminently capable in the social realm of dinner parties and flowers, Lesly's truth strengths rest in her reach beyond the island. Working with her family, she carries on her mother's work in the social services, responding to the unmet needs of the homeless and unemployed.

As a political force, her leadership of the town through its strong periods of growth showed an understanding of urban redevelopment and civic responsibility. Both were mayors of the Town of Palm Beach: Earl (1971-1977) and Lesly (2000-2005).

PHOTO CREDIT: Bob Davidoff

Dorothy Sullivan

PHOTO CREDIT: Devine

Born and breed in Boston, Dorothy Sullivan spent her early professional career sharing her educational background in chemistry with high school students and worked as a chemist at the Lahey Clinic.

Dorothy recognized the necessary components to bring people and causes together and brought her education to play in the non-profit world. Recognized for her tireless efforts in fundraising for organizations meeting the needs of the sick and the needy, Dorothy came to Palm Beach and founded Angels of Charity in addition to serving the Palm Beach Opera Guild, Home Safe for Abused Children, WXEL, Hope House and other community-centered activities.

A woman of faith, she has shared her passions with many for the good of all. Her lively personality added immeasurably to the events she chaired and the younger charity-minded individuals she mentored for the next generation of Palm Beach angels.

PHOTO CREDIT: Bob Davidoff

Donald J. Trump

Considered the most high-profile resident, wherever he may live, Donald Trump could well be called the quintessential Renaissance man for the breadth and depth of his endeavors over the last five decades. Realtor, developer, golfer, author, producer, promoter – each field brought Trump to an even higher level of expertise and respect in the business community – and the world. With the opening of the Grand Hyatt in 1980, he was identified as New York's most well-known and controversial developer.

While some might consider placing his name on every project at bit showy, Trump knows the value of branding and builds his projects to the highest of standards – precisely because their bear his name. His father's early mentoring in building and construction laid the foundation for a career his father would later say some of '[the] best deals were made by my son".

His purchase in 1985 of the Post Estate, Mar-a-Lago set the Town of Palm Beach on its heels. Having sat empty for over a decade, the jewel of Palm Beach had a master craftsman ready to breathe new life and glamour to the fabled mansion. Trump studied the territory, determined he had the best opportunity to make Palm Beach a truly international destination, one free of prejudice, open to celebrations and responsible in preservation. The Mar-a-Lago Club was created and recaptured the very essence of Marjorie Merriweather Post's royal palace. Grand events, well-known celebrities and charitable events came back to Palm Beach. The legacy of Mar-a-Lago continues.

Donald J. Trump is an American success story. He has continually set new standards of excellence while expanding his interests nationally and internationally. His commitment has made him the pre-eminent developer of quality real estate known around the world. The Trump gold standard is apparent in all his endeavors. He is the quintessential businessman—a deal-maker without peer, with an eye to value and productivity and an ardent philanthropist.

PHOTO CREDIT: Lucien Capehart

Donald Trump being interviewed in the white and gold ballroom of his private Mar-a-lago Club during the Palm Beach Centennial opening night, April 15th, 2011.

PHOTO CREDIT: Lucien Capehart

Kathryn and Leo Vecellio

The Vecellio family was once described with a tagline reading, "all good things to all good people." With their family company, The Vecellio Group, founded in 1938 by Leo's father, a fourth generation now stands ready to carry its mission forward. The company offers a wide range of highway, mining and energy services and products around the country.

As a result of the The Vecellio Group's success, the Vecellio Family Foundation was created to meet the educational needs of deserving students from the communities served by the company, and the children of its employees. To date, the Vecellio Family Foundation has awarded thousands of dollars and over 333 scholarships to students in Florida, West Virginia and North Carolina. The family also supports many colleges, universities and organizations, in addition to numerous health care and research institutions.

"We believe in the value of a good education and in giving back to the communities where our company has its roots," reported Mr. Vecellio. "My wife, our sons and I believe in contributing to the communities our company serves, and to the support of our employees' families."

Mr. Vecellio, who has chaired the Palm Beach Economic Council and the American Road and Transportation Builders Association, has been a member of the prestigious Florida Council of 100, the Florida Transportation Builders Association and the Virginia Tech Foundation Board.

Following in the tradition of Palm Beach's great ladies who worked tirelessly on charity events from the early 1920s, Kathryn Vecellio has, for the past 37 years, demonstrated an unconquerable spirit of leadership and philanthropy in support of charitable events benefiting a wide range of interests. The arts, health and human services, medicine, and science have been touched by her strong organizational skills, fundraising expertise, passion for service and knowledge of the current needs and concerns of the community.

The American Heart Association, American Red Cross, Cleveland Clinic, Schepens Eye Research Institute/Mass. Eye and Ear, Kravis Center for the Performing Arts, Leukemia & Lymphoma Society, Norton Museum of Art, South Florida Science Center, Junior League of the Palm Beaches and the Daughters of the American Revolution have all enjoyed Mrs. Vecellio's service, and can all attest to her indefatigable commitment and unprecedented support and success at raising funds on their behalf.

Since 1979, Mr. and Mrs. Vecellio have both have been presented with countless awards from national, regional and Palm Beach charitable organizations. Their incredible generosity to community, family, church and charities exemplifies their extraordinary spirit of giving and their love for the community.

The Duke and Duchess of Windsor

They were an international sensation when he abdicated the throne of England for the woman he loved – and married. She set a new standard for fashion. They traveled the world but had no real destinations…until they made their first trip to Palm Beach in 1941 and returned for the next 30 years.

The Palm Beach 'season' grew from Flagler's day when it ran from New Year's to Washington's birthday. Then there was the "Windsor Season" – also known as the 'little season'. Seasonal residents would put off closing their homes when told of their eminent arrival, such was their appeal as social arbiters. Everyone wanted to entertain The Duke and Duchess who arrived by train, along with a freight car filled with luggage and their beloved dogs.

PHOTO CREDIT: Bob Davidoff

Charities and Organizations

Recognition and memories are preserved through the tireless efforts of our philanthropic organizations and publications. They have captured the history of lives transformed through giving by having made a difference. They serve as a constant reminder of our role in responding to humanity. **Laurel Baker**

Some people dream of making a difference… Palm Beachers have made it a skill. **Olympia Devine**

American Heart Association

The Palm Beach Heart Ball is the American Heart Association's longest running and most successful Heart Gala in the country, raising more money than all others, which goes directly to fighting heart disease and stroke. Each year the ball is held during February, proclaimed nationally as American Heart Month back in the early 1960s.

1956 - Perry Como and Dinah Shore in promo shots for the inaugurial Palm Beach Heart Ball, February 14th, 1956.

The Palm Beach Heart Ball's history began on Valentine's Day, February 14, 1956, held at The Patio with Lucius Pond Ordway serving as inaugural chairman. Gypsy Rose Lee pulled the winning raffle ticket for a '56 Ford Thunderbird, and Jacqueline Leslie was crowned "Miss Heart." Anna Thompson Dodge, widow of the automotive magnate Horace E. Dodge and Florence Pritchett, wife of Palm Beach Mayor Earl E.T. Smith, served on the special heart fund and ticket committees for the gala. Tickets were $25 and the event raised a very impressive $40,840 for the American Heart Association.

The 1957 Palm Beach Heart Ball was moved to the Poinciana Room of the Palm Beach Towers hotel (converted to a condominium in 1974). High-profile guests included Senator John F. and Jackie Kennedy; Joseph P. Kennedy, Sr. and his wife, Rose; long- time Palm Beach resident and president of the New York Yankees, Dan Topping who brought Joe DiMaggio; Rita Moreno; Ann Miller and Anita Ekberg.

In 1958, television star Ed Sullivan served as the master of ceremonies for the ball, Mamie Eisenhower was Honorary National Chairman and renowned artist Norman Rockwell painted the commemorative poster.

In 2008, under the distinctive leadership of Chairman Mrs. Kathryn C. Vecellio, the 53rd Annual Palm Beach Heart Ball, "Valentines at Versailles," achieved unprecedented success, standing to date as the most financially successful gala in the event's history, raising more than $2 million.

Through the Decades at the Annual Palm Beach Heart Ball

1966
Actress Joan Crawford, Louis Marron and Mary Nemac.

1970
Jack Eckard presents heart transplant surgeon, Dr. Christian Barnard, with an award.

1983
Evelyn Swartz and actor Peter Falk of TV series Columbo.

2008
Kathryn C. Vecellio, whose efforts led to the most successful Heart Ball in the nation.

2009
Miss America 2009, Katie Stam, an honored guest.

2011
Burt Reynolds, Honorary Heart Ambassador for 2011.

Palm Beach Heart Ball Event Chairmen

1956 - Mr. Lucius Pond Ordway
1957 - Mrs. Horace Dodge, Jr.
1958 - Mrs. Lorraine Freimann
- Mr. Christopher Dunphy
1959 - Mrs. Frank McMahon
1960 - Mrs. Carleton Dodge
1961 - Mrs. O. Roy Chalk
1962 - Mrs. Benson Ford
1963 - Mrs. Carleton Dodge
1964 - Mrs. Homer H. Marshman
1965 - Mrs. Harry C. Mills
1966 - Mrs. Louis E. Marron
1967 - Mrs. Roy Tuchbreiter
1968 - Mrs. Albin Holder
1969 - Mrs. Robert Sonquist
1970 - Mrs. Arthur A. Burck
1971 - Mrs. Peter I.B. Lavan
- Mrs. Conrad Thibault
1972 - Mrs. E. Llwyd Eccelstone, Sr.
1973 - Mrs. Edward G. FitzHenry
1974 - Mrs. John H. Tripp
1975 - Mrs. Kenneth P. Richter
1976 - Mrs. Douglas Payne
1977 - Mrs. Hans F. Fischer
1978 - Mrs. Alexander G. Stone
1979 - Mrs. Harry E. Houghton
1980 - Mrs. Jack Hight
1981 - Mrs. James I. Adams
1982 - Mrs. H. Richard Williams
1983 - Mrs. Howard R. Swartz
1984 - Mrs. Robert G. Hurbaugh
1985 - Mrs. Hunter S. Marston, Jr.
1986 - Mrs. Rolla D. Campbell, Jr.
1987 - Mrs. Clother H. Vaughn III
1988 - Mrs. Theodore T. Tarone
1989 - Mrs. Betty M. Martin
1990 - Mrs. Robert C. Salisbury
1991 - Mrs. Florenz Ourisman
1992 - Mrs. Curt E. Gowdy
1993 - Mrs. Walter M. Ross
1994 - Mrs. Kathlyn Maguire
1995 - Mrs. William L. Kemp, Jr.
1996 - Mrs. Judith M. Grubman
1997 - Mrs. Victor J. Scaravilli
1998 - Mrs. Peter A. Dupuis
1999 - Mrs. John E. Nicolo
2000 - Mrs. E. Llwyd Ecclestone
2001 - Mrs. Dick Robinson
2002 - Mrs. Simon C. Fireman
2003 - Mrs. Alton J. O'Neil
2004 - Mrs. Robert G. Gordon
2005 - Mrs. Curt E. Gowdy
- Mrs. Kathlyn Maguire
- Mrs. William L. Kemp, Jr.
- Mrs. Judith M. Grubman
- Mrs. Victor J. Scaravilli
- Mrs. Peter A. Dupuis
- Mrs. Dick Robinson
- Mrs. Simon C. Fireman
- Mrs. Alton J. O'Neil
- Mrs. Robert G. Gordon
- Mrs. Clother H. Vaughn III
- Mrs. Theodore T. Tarone
2006 - Mr. Patrick Park
- Ms. Mary Fairbanks
2007 - Mrs. Sydell L. Miller
2008 - Mrs. Kathryn Vecellio
2009 - Mrs. Elizabeth M. Bowden
- Mrs. Arlette B. Gordon
2010 - Mrs. Melania Trump
- Mrs. Petra Levin
2011 - Mrs. Lois Pope
2012 - Mrs. Paula Butler
2013 - Mrs. Hermé de Wyman Miro
- Mrs. Veronica Atkins
2014 - Mrs. Julie Rudolph
2015 - Founders' Circle Members

More than 2,200 Americans die of cardiovascular diseases each day — one person every 39 seconds. Research is a major weapon in the fight against these diseases. Since 1949, the American Heart Association has spent more than $3.4 billion on research to increase knowledge about cardiovascular diseases and stroke. Last year alone, the American Heart Association funded nearly $130 million in lifesaving research projects. Currently, there are 58 active grants in the state of Florida totaling $9,328,664. The American Heart Association is second only to the federal government in funding cardiovascular and stroke research. Over the years, the always elegant Palm Beach Heart Ball has become known as one of the premier events of the social season. Most importantly, the event has established itself as a driving force in advancing the key initiatives of the American Heart Association, including significantly combating heart disease and stroke, the No.1 and No. 4 killers of men and women in the United States.

In addition, the Association raises awareness of heart disease as the number one killer of women, with its Go Red For Women initiative, designed to empower women to take charge of their heart health. Kathryn Vecellio is the Palm Beach founding member of the Go Red for Women Founders Circle. The Go Red For Women initiative finds ways to help ensure heart disease and stroke are more widely recognized and treated. www.heart.org

The American Red Cross

PHOTO CREDIT: Lucien Capehart

The South Florida Region of the American Red Cross is part of the largest humanitarian relief organization in the United States. For almost 100 years, the local Red Cross has given hope and help to people in their greatest hour of need – meeting the physical and emotional needs of disaster victims, teaching lifesaving skills such as CPR and first aid, and supporting military members and their families. The American Red Cross prevents and alleviates human suffering in the face of emergencies by mobilizing the power of volunteers and the generosity of donors.

Although the Red Cross is not a government agency, it is an essential part of the response when disaster strikes. The Red Cross works in partnership with other agencies and organizations that provide services to disaster victims.

Beverly White Yeager and Mary Mochary - 2013

Kathryn C. Vecellio - 2014

Mary Ourisman, Bonnie McElveen-Hunter and Gail McGovern - 2013

The leading special event fundraiser supporting the local work of the Red Cross is the International Red Cross Ball. The International Red Cross Ball is a white-tie and tiara affair, welcoming ambassadors, dignitaries and philanthropic leaders from around the world in celebration of all that the American Red Cross does for our community and beyond. What began as a very small party has become the premier social event of the Palm Beach season. Established by Marjorie Merriweather Post in 1957, the ball has raised millions of dollars for the American Red Cross.

A fire in the Red Cross Chapter office at Morrison Field, now Palm Beach International Airport, destroyed a good portion on the chapter's archives. Because the press took little notice of the Red Cross fundraiser until the early 1960s, what is known about the earliest years of the ball is drawn from the memories of those involved.

The office is now located at 1250 Northpoint Parkway in West Palm Beach and can be found online at www.redcross.org.

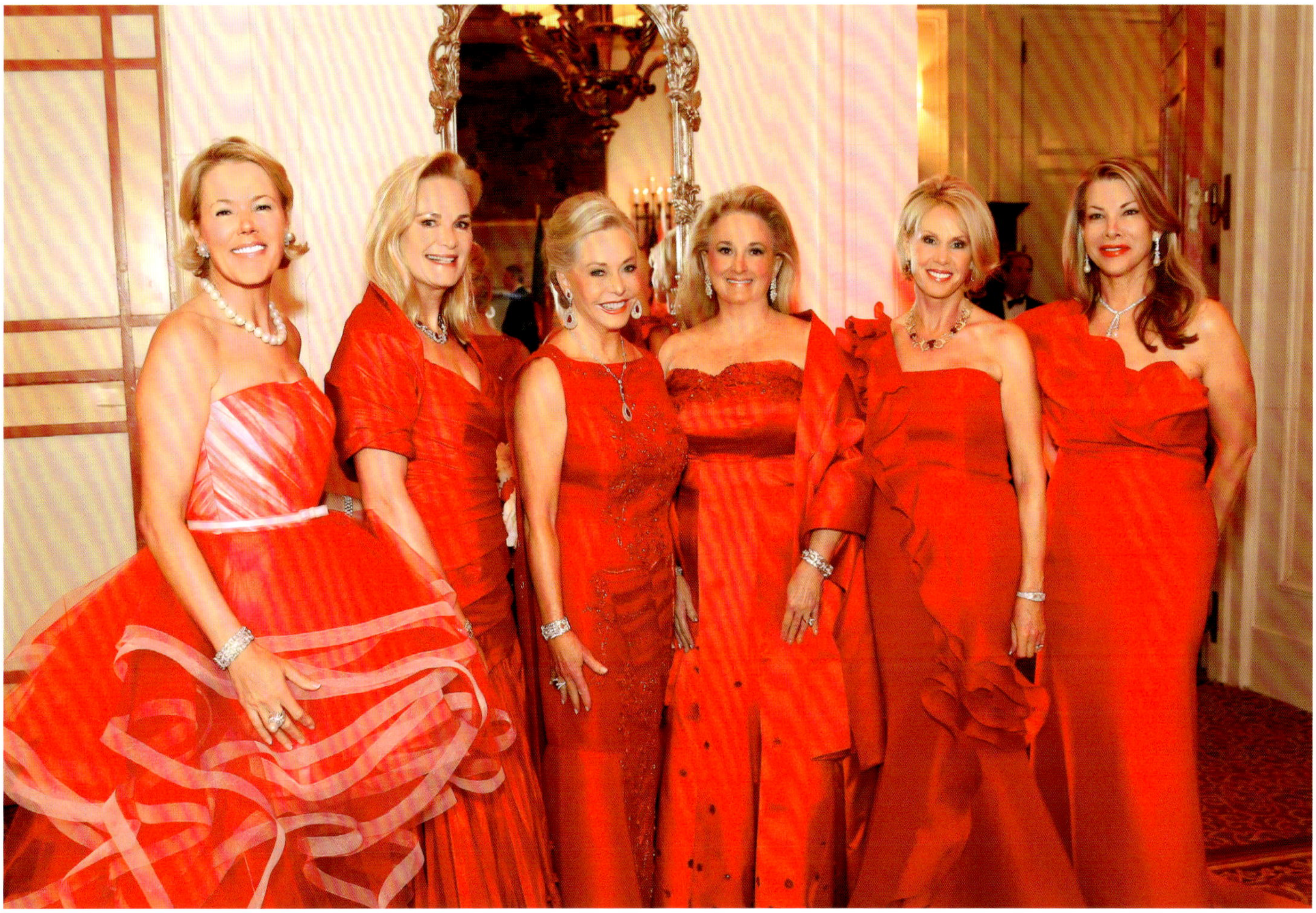

Rhonda Wilkins, Paula Butler, Mary Ourisman, Kathryn Vecellio, Trish Donnelley and Amanda Schumacher - 2013

International Red Cross Ball Chairmen/Women

1957 - 1960 - Helen Rankin & Martha Rankin

1961 - Lorraine Salisbury

1962 - 1963 - Claire Wheeler

1964 - Anne White

1965 - Helene Tuchbreiter

1966 - Lorraine Colvin

1967 - Faye Lavan

1968 - 1972 - Celeste Cheatham

1973 - 1993 - Sue Whitmore

1994 - Richard & Jacqueline Cowell

1995 - Jean Tailer

1996 - 1998 - Betty Scripps

1999 - Candace Van Alen

2000 - Betty Scripps

2001 - 2004 - Diana Eccelstone

2005 - 2006 - Simon Fireman

2007 - 2009 - Bill & Nancy Rollnick

2010 - 2011 - Michele Kessler

2012 - 2013 - Mary Ourisman

2014 - Kathryn Vecellio

The Center for Family Services of Palm Beach County

"Strengthening families through counseling, education and homeless intervention."

The Center for Family Services is a non-profit, social services organization whose mission is strengthening families through counseling, education and homeless intervention. The agency provides a full spectrum of services for homeless families with children and families at risk for homelessness; substance abuse treatment programs; as well as specialized therapy for children who are victims of sexual abuse and domestic violence.

History:

Efforts to establish a Family Agency in this community date back to 1945. Serious efforts were made in 1960, when a group representing every private, public, social and welfare organization in the count realized the need for this basic community service and decided to sponsor a Family Service Steering Committee. This committee felt that the first step would be to document the need, and distributed more than 3,000 questionnaires to all agencies, schools, doctors, lawyers, judges, ministers – in fact everyone who dealt with people and their daily problems. One of the questions asked was, "How many people have you seen in the past 12 months who needed some kind of family counseling?" The replies were staggering, as you can see –

3,160 needed Marriage Counseling

4,215 needed Parent-Child Guidance

1,700 needed Job Adjustment Help

5,415 needed help in Planning for the Mentally or Physically Ill

4,300 needed help with Problems of the Aged

7,900 needed help in Budgeting and Home Management

3,900 needed Counseling in Individual Personal Problems

With this overwhelming evidence and the total lack of counseling service, the next two years were spent in trying to educate the community to the need. In 1961, The Center received their charter for Palm Beach County. A board was created with several members who were social workers. They were very generous in contributing as much of their time as they could spare. Ministers, lawyers, doctors, and other agencies also helped by seeing these troubled people.

Patty Myura with children in front of The Pat Reeves Village Homeless Shelter in West Palm Beach

In 1971, the name of the agency was officially changed from the Family Service Agency to the Family Counseling Center. In 1973, the agency employed, in West Palm Beach, three and a half social workers and the Boca Raton office continued on a part-time basis with three part-time social workers until September 1, 1973, when that office was opened on a full time basis. The year of 1973 was seen as a year of agency stabilization. In 1978, the agency's name was changed to The Center for Family Services. In February, 1987, the agency celebrated its 25th Anniversary with a dinner and awards ceremony at the Royce Hotel. In 1991, The Center had its most successful Dinner Dance to date. That was followed in April with another successful Child Abuse Luncheon. Also, due to the generosity of Jack and Barbara Nicklaus, along with the help of the PGA and Golden Bear International, the agency participated in the "Jack Nicklaus Challenge for Charity." This year also resulted in greater publicity and success in fundraising due to the Dinner Dance, Child Abuse Luncheon, "Home for the Holidays" and Channel 5's "Beat the Pro".

Patty Myura

Seated Left to Right : First Row - Amy Guerrieri, Kitty Silverstein, Arlette Gordon, Patricia Myura, Lauren Kesselman and Karen Swanson. Second Row seated - Lisa Erdmann and Amie Swan. Standing - Sherry Walker Borchert , Sonja Stevens, Erin McGould, Stanton Collemer, Joan Klann, Melissa Parker and Patricia Travis.

It wasn't until 1998 when The Center for Family Services launched the Old Bags Luncheon™ which is today one of the largest fundraising luncheons in Palm Beach County. Now in its sixteenth year, the event attracts over 600 of Palm Beach's most philanthropic women, ranging in age from their 20's to their 80's. Proceeds directly benefit programs for families and children in crisis in our community providing therapy to adult and child victims of domestic violence, sexual abuse and/or other crimes, and shelter to homeless families with children. The agency provides critical life-changing services to more than 15,000 individuals and families annually.

In 2000, Patty's dream was fulfilled when she and her friends donated funds to build what is now known as The Pat Reeve Village Emergency Shelter, the only emergency shelter in Palm Beach County for families with children.

Today, the shelter located in West Palm Beach serves 30-40 children a night. Patty Myura was one of the founders of Old Bags Luncheon™. Patty knew The Center had a homeless shelter and out of curiosity wanted to visit the "Rock Garden Motel." After visiting the shelter, Patty was on a mission to improve and build a new facility. www.ctrfam.org

George Hamilton

Regis Philbin

Debbie Reynolds

Joan Rivers

Celebrities who have spoken at the Old Bags Luncheon™ throughout the years

Eleanor Patterson Reeves and the Reeves Foundation

Eleanor Patterson Reeves was a woman of refinement, education and sophistication. She traveled the world, entertained and engaged in a variety of activities suited to her station in life. But her true vision was far removed from the life she led. With the creation of the Eleanor Patterson Reeves Foundation, a world of opportunity opened for the under-privileged and under-served in the local community.

With the guidance of **Patty Myura,** foundation president, Mrs. Reeves' interests in supporting the needy became a reality. Among the most notable project is **Pat Reeves Village, operated by the Center for Family Services.**

Mosaic of the "Providencia" Shipwreck 1878. The Preservation Foundation Office 311 Peruvian Avenue

The Palm Beach Preservation Foundation

"The Preservation Foundation of Palm Beach is a nonprofit organization dedicated to preserving the unique environment of the Town of Palm Beach and to educating residents about our special heritage.

We are a locally organized private group with a board of trustees who resides in the community. The Preservation Foundation fulfills its goals through a variety of well-tested programs.

The Preservation Foundation interacts with the town government to support programs and policies that encourage preservation of Palm Beach's historic architecture and maintenance of the residential quality of our landmarks. Property tax abatement for historic landmarks, accurate appraisal information for historic homes and consultant studies for management of redevelopment pressures are among the public issue campaigns the Preservation Foundation has funded."
Courtesy of www.palmbeachguide.com

www.palmbeachpreservation.org

Citizens' Association of Palm Beach

(l-r) Alan Golboro, Jimmy Ryan, Alan Horwitz, Rodney Blair, Lee Goldstein, Bob Keats, Harold Epstein, Rita Taca, Bernard Panfel, Roberta Mambrino, Lew Crampton, Jane Waldman, (behind Jane) Donald Singer, Ellen Tansey, Dan McDonnell, Jack Cohen, Bill King, Jerry Frank and Bruce M. Heyman

Our Association was created by residents south of Sloan's Curve more than 38 years ago. We work to protect, preserve and improve the area in which we live and work. The Citizens' Association represents approximately 6,000 residents in 53 condominiums, co-op buildings, single family homes, along with interested residents in the Town of Palm Beach.

2875 South Ocean Boulevard, Suite 200
www.citizensassociationofpalmbeach.org

The Palm Beach Civic Association

The Palm Beach Civic Association was founded in 1944 by a handful of civic minded Palm Beachers who wished to preserve, protect and enhance the special qualities of their amazing island. Under the leadership of John F. Gunster, first Civic Association president, and the founder of the first law firm in Palm Beach, and famous Palm Beach architect John Volk, PBCA secretary, the association quickly grew its membership to over 300 members in the first two years.

Executive Committee member Alan Miller, Honorary members Dick Raffo, Lewis Schott, and Harriet Miller

Chairman Emeritus Louis Pryor and Executive Committee member E. Llwyd Ecclestone

For decades, the Civic Association has been guided by great leaders such as Bob Wright, Stephen L. Brown, William M. Guttman, George G. Matthews, Louis C. Pryor, Doyle Rogers, Stanley M. Rumbough, Jr. and Harold B. Scott. The membership has grown to well over 2,000 men and women. A prestigious board of 130 directors guides the active community organization and more than 90 Palm Beach businesses are corporate members.

Chairmen Emeriti George Matthews and Stanley M. Rumbough, Jr.

Chairman Emeritus Doyle Rogers and Kathryn Vecellio

Executive Committee member
Michele Kessler and Howard Kessler

Suzanne Wright, Chairman and CEO Bob Wright, Andrea Mitchel,
Director James Patterson and Sue Patterson

Today, the Palm Beach Civic Association continues to embody the same basic principles that it was founded on almost a century ago.

- Protect and improve the quality of life in Palm Beach
- Educate and engage residents on key town issues
- Take proactive stands on civic affairs
- Work closely with local government
- Encourage citizen involvement in this amazing community

Preserving Palm Beach is the heart of the Civic Association's mission. We share a never-ending passion for this one-of-a-kind community. Our directors, members, and corporate partners stand proudly with others throughout the generations in making Palm Beach the very best place to call home.

For more information on becoming a member of the Palm Beach Civic Association, please call 561-655-0820 or contact us at www.PalmBeachCivic.org

Executive Committee member Dave Duffy and Tom Brokow

Executive Committee member William Matthews, Jean Matthews
and Executive Committee member Bob Nederlander

GUNSTER

Palm Beach's First Law Firm

l-r: Marshall M. Criser, Joseph F. Gunster and George W. Hersey III

Back in 1942, when Gunster founder John Kenneth Williamson decided to open the first law office in Palm Beach, there were some who may have questioned the wisdom of such a plan. At the time, the winter season was short and most of Palm Beach's prominent residents relied on their northern attorneys for legal counsel.

Williamson, however, had correctly anticipated a growing population and longer season. In the ensuing decades, under the direction of Williamson and co-founders Joseph F. Gunster and Buck Baugher, the firm's relationship with Palm Beach deepened and flourished. Today, although the island is home to 135 attorneys and 25 banks, Gunster retains its community leadership roles and deep knowledge of Palm Beach and the needs of its residents.

Known for his "simple and straightforward" manner, which is well chronicled in local history, Williamson was quick to help anyone with a problem and put his skills to work for organizations such as Good Samaritan Hospital and the Palm Beach Community Chest. His partner, Joe Gunster, a native of Scranton, Pennsylvania, quickly established himself as a community leader, serving as president of the Palm Beach Civic Association and of the Society of the Four Arts, the island's premier cultural institution. Each of these institutions continues to enjoy the support of the firm and its attorneys to this day.

The partners and associates who built the firm through its first two decades, including David "Bud" Yoakley, Marshall Criser, Obie Stewart and George William Hersey, shared the founders' passion for civic and community involvement. Criser, who served as the president of the Florida Bar and later, as president of the University of Florida from 1985 to 1989. Locally, he was the chairman of the board for several prominent charitable organizations. And even in a community renowned around the country for its philanthropic feats, the considerable work of George Hersey,

1968 dinner party at Joseph F. Gunster's home. Standing left to right: George W. Hersey III, Peter Van Andel, David S. "Bud" Yoakley, Joseph F. Gunster, A. Obie Stewart and Robert T. Scott. Seated left to right: Marshall M. Criser, Kenneth S. Beall, Jr., Dennis W. Hiller.

with the Community Chest, the Palm Beach Community Foundation and the Palm Beach Mental Health Center, among other organizations — stands out.

As the law firm of Gunster continued to grow in size, reputation and influence in the latter half of the 20th century, it never lost sight of its long-standing commitment to Palm Beach and its residents. Several of the firm's attorneys, including Daniel Hanley and Kenneth S. Beall, Jr., have been Palm Beach residents for decades and each have a deep connection to the island and the greater Palm Beach community. Over the years, the firm has represented several of the island's iconic institutions, such as The Breakers Hotel, while its attorneys have always lent their support to the area's most beloved charitable organizations, including The Historical Society of Palm Beach County, Hospice of Palm Beach County, The Rehabilitation Center for Children and Adults and the Community Foundation for Palm Beach and Martin Counties.

Gunster's Palm Beach Office, 151 Royal Palm Way. Drawing by Paige Pressly.

Today, Gunster employs nearly 400 attorneys and staff, has offices in every major city in the state, and is known as one of the most respected commercial law firms in the Southeast. The firm's primary practice areas include: private wealth services, real estate, tax, business litigation, banking and financial services, healthcare, environmental and land use, government affairs, construction, and employment and labor.

Yet, despite the firm's impressive growth and statewide expansion, its roots remain firmly embedded in Palm Beach, and its culture continues to spring from the same gracious gentility and philanthropic spirit that defines the island. As Hanley notes, "The sense of connectivity between the firm and Palm Beach is something very real that was passed to us from our founders. We are passionate about sharing and cultivating it with the next generation of attorneys at the firm. That is the cornerstone of the Gunster legacy in Palm Beach."
www.gunster.com

The International Society of Palm Beach

Hermé de Wyman Miro often refers to The International Society of Palm Beach as her "Labor of Love". The International Society of Palm Beach has the dedicated purpose to make a difference in the lives of many by giving something back to our community.

The International Society of Palm Beach distributes scholarships and grants by supporting the arts, fostering education, furthering medicine and research, support child welfare, animal welfare and other humanitarian causes.

The International Society of Palm Beach consists of internationally minded people whose interests and tastes are similar and who enjoy each other's company at the Society's varied and interesting functions. This wonderful organization was founded by Herme de Wyman Miro and her late husband, Rene De Wyman.

Thanks to Hermé de Wyman Miro's devotion and untiring fundraising efforts, The International Society of Palm beach has been able to distribute many grants and scholarships to worthy charities totaling many millions of dollars.

Hermé de Wyman together with her husband René, founded the International Society of Palm Beach in 1983 and she has been its Founding President ever since. Her marriage to her beloved first husband lasted 54 years. René de Wyman predeceased her in 1991.

Hermé de Wyman with her second husband, David M. Miro, a prominent attorney from Michigan who supported all of her dedicated community efforts.

For more information on The International Society of Palm Beach, please call (561) 832-4200.

The following charities are some of many who have benefited from it's Founder, President Herme de Wyman Miro's hardwork, devotion and the generosity of the Society's Great Grand Benefactors, Grand Benefactors and Patrons:

Achilles International
Adopt- A-Family of the Palm Beaches
Alzheimer's Association Southeast Chapter
Alzheimer's Community Care
American Ballet Theatre
American Cancer Society
R.O.C.K Reaching Out to Cancer Kids
American Friends of Magen David Adom
American Heart Association
American Humane Association
American Red Cross Palm Beach County Chapter
American Lung Association
Arthur R. Marshall Foundation
ASPCA
Bascom Palmer Eye Institute
Brigham and Women's Hospital
Camp Boggy Creek
Cardinal Newman High School
Career Transition for Dancers
Center for Family Services
Children's Home Society
Cleveland Clinic
Club 100 Charities
Covenant House
The Crystal Ball
Cystic Fibrosis Foundation
Dana Farber Cancer Institute
Families First of Palm Beach County
Food for the Poor
Friends of AKIM, USA
Gift of Life Bone Marrow Foundation
God's Creatures Big & Small
Israel Cancer Association USA
Historical Society of Palm Beach
Hospice of Palm Beach County
Institute of Laryngology
Israel Cancer Association USA
Junior Achievement of the Palm Beaches
Jupiter Medical Center -Foundation Breast Center
Kids Sanctuary Campus
LIFE Leaders in Furthering Education
Leukemia & Lymphoma Society Palm Beach Area Chapter
The Lord's Place
Lupus Foundation of America
Lynn University

Raymond F. Kravis Center for the Performing Arts

School programming

Harris Pre-function Hall

Through diverse programming and a resolve to remain a thriving not-for-profit education and outreach facility accessible to everyone, the Raymond F. Kravis Center for the Performing Arts has established itself as a leading force in the social fabric of Palm Beach County. Its mission is to enhance the quality of life in the community by presenting a diverse schedule of national and international artists and companies of the highest order; by offering comprehensive arts education programs; by providing a home in which local and regional arts organizations can showcase their work; and by providing economic catalyst and community leadership in West Palm Beach, supporting efforts to increase travel and tourism to Palm Beach County.

The Kravis Center complex

Dreyfoos Concert Hall

Each season the Center stages approximately 550 shows that are attended by nearly half a million people. It opened in 1992 and is a multipurpose facility featuring four performance venues, the 2,195-seat Dreyfoos Concert Hall, the 300-seat Rinker Playhouse, the 300-seat Persson Hall and the outdoor Gosman Amphitheatre with a capacity for 1,400 patrons.

The Center's Cohen Pavilion houses the Weiner Banquet Center, Gimelstob Ballroom and Harris Pre-function Hall. It also houses the Picower Foundation Arts Education Center and the Elmore Family Business Center for the Arts. Food service is provided by Catering by The Breakers at the Kravis Center. www.kravis.org

Gimelstob Ballroom

The Lois Pope Life Foundation, Inc.

Lois Pope is one of America's leading philanthropists and humanitarians. Through the Lois Pope LIFE Foundation, Inc. and LIFE (Leaders in Furthering Education), she is devoted to saving lives, helping people help themselves, improving the quality of life for families in need and encouraging young Americans to become leaders by helping others. Her foundations have also provided awards for medical research, college scholarships, humanitarian relief, the performing arts, and animal welfare. In December of 2013, Lois Pope, LIFE and the LIFE Foundation, Inc., celebrated 20 years of dedication to helping those in need at the 20th Annual "Lady in Red" Gala.

In 1996, when Lois Pope announced a $10 million gift to the University of Miami to establish the Lois Pope LIFE Center and fund 20 LIFE Fellows per year for neurological research, she knew it was much more than a gift, it was a promise. "In 1994, my good friend Christopher Reeve was the guest of honor at the LIFE's fundraising gala. I danced with Chris that evening. Three months later, he was paralyzed. Chris so inspired me with his courage and his faith that I was resolved to help further spinal cord research. We continue to search for a cure for paralysis through our efforts at the Lois Pope LIFE Center" said Mrs. Pope.

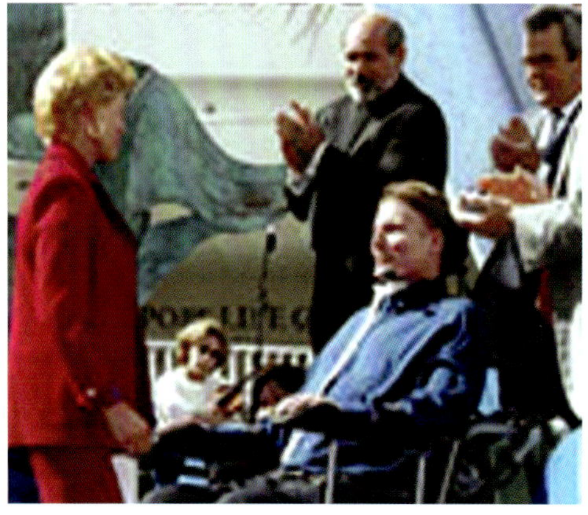

The generous commitment was the largest private gift of its kind to support spinal cord research and it was a promise that the end of paralysis would be found within the walls of the Lois Pope LIFE Center. Because of Mrs. Pope's generosity and the diligence of LIFE Center Scientists, the most significant advances in spinal cord research of the late 20th and early 21st century have been discovered within the LIFE Center walls.

The Lois Pope LIFE Center is now the top catastrophic neurological research facility in the world and home to the renowned Miami Project to Cure Paralysis.

Lois Pope gives five ambulances to American Friends of Magen David Adom (AFMDA)

Lois Pope has given five ambulances to American Friends of Magen David Adom (AFMDA) for the life-saving purposes of Magen David Adom in Israel. Thanks to Lois Pope and AFMDA supporters like her, more than 800 MDA standard ambulances and Mobile Intensive Cardiac Care Units ambulances are on call 24/7, operating from over 100 Emergency Medical Stations and 11 dispatch stations throughout Israel, logging more than 9.775 million miles and taking care of more than 520,000 patients annually. The ambulances are manufactured in the United States and are designed to meet the needs of Israel's demanding requirements.

Disabled Veterans' LIFE
Memorial Foundation

Lois Pope co-founded the Disabled Veterans' LIFE Memorial Foundation to spearhead development of the American Veterans Disabled for Life Memorial, the nation's first and only permanent public tribute to the three million living disabled American veterans and the countless others who have died. The memorial is being constructed near the US Capitol and will commemorate the sacrifices and dedication of disabled American veterans from all branches of the Armed Services throughout America's history. A dedication is set for Fall 2014.

Lois Pope Red Star Rescue Vehicle

In 2012, Lois Pope and LIFE joined in partnership with American Humane Association (AHA), to create a program to protect the voiceless and the vulnerable in our society - abused and neglected animals. The Lois Pope Red Star Rescue Vehicle was dedicated in the spring of 2013 in Palm Beach and within hours of the devastation caused by tornadoes in Moore, Oklahoma, this vehicle was deployed to help animals in need. A second Lois Pope Red Star Rescue Vehicle for the northeastern United States was added in October 2013, expanding the reach of AHA services even further. www.life-edu.org

Palm Beach Daily News

Covering life on the island for more than a century

by Darrell Hofheinz

In 1910, the staff of the *Palm Beach Daily News* and *Palm Beach Life* was composed of five people, including Publisher Richard Overend Davies (in the white suit and boater's cap) and Ruby Edna Pierce (center), who joined the paper in 1907 as a cashier and then held the position of editor and general manager for more than 40 years. *Photo courtesy of Historical Society of Palm Beach County*

The *Palm Beach Daily News* – affectionately known as "The Shiny Sheet" because of its high-quality newsprint – has served as a chronicle of all things Palm Beach for more than a century. The newspaper dates to 1897, when America's elite journeyed to Palm Beach in private railroad cars to stay at Henry Flagler's Hotel Royal Poinciana or The Breakers. They got their news from one source. The *Palm Beach Daily News* has grown up alongside the town, chronicling its evolution from the hotel and "Cottage Colony" era – through booms and slowdowns – to the present day.

The newspaper and its website, PalmBeachDailyNews.com, are known for their wide-ranging and in-depth coverage of topics of interest to readers who live and play in one of the wealthiest areas in the United States. Articles focus on society news, charitable events and organizations, local government, business, real estate, fashion, local history, the arts and entertainment. The publishing schedule includes *Palm Beach Life* magazine, which celebrated its centennial in 2006.

Owned by Cox Enterprises since 1969, the *Palm Beach Daily News* is part of Cox Media Group. The newspaper publishes daily from early October to late May and twice a week during the summer months. But the website and digital products are updated daily year-round.

The *Palm Beach Daily News* is truly a one-of-a-kind medium devoted to a one-of-a-kind community.

An undated photograph shows the *Palm Beach Daily News* building on South County Road at Brazilian Avenue. Built in 1925, the landmarked building was the newspaper's home until the early 1970s. It is listed in the National Register of Historic Places

This undated photograph was used in a promotional campaign for the *Palm Beach Daily News*

PHOTO CREDIT: Jeffrey Langlois, 2013

For the 75th anniversary in 1972, paper dresses were made from copies of the *Palm Beach Daily News*

SUMMER REVAMP

HEROES

ECOPARK

Palm Beach Daily News

Managers: Playhouse safe from bulldozer

Addison Mizner-designed park

A HISTORY OF CHANGE

PALM BEACH DAILY NEWS

THE CHILDREN'S COTILLION WAS AN IMPORTANT EVENT

PALM BEACH IS VERY POPULAR MANY GUESTS AT BOTH HOTELS

The *Palm Beach Daily News* as it appears today, at left, and as it looked in 1905.

Palm Beach Daily News Timeline

1894 - Alabama native S. Bobo Dean forms the Dean Publishing Co. and with his brother Joel launches *The Weekly Lake Worth News* in West Palm Beach.

1897 - The *Palm Beach Daily News* is born, although under a different name: The Deans begin publishing The *Daily Lake Worth News,* a seasonal publication printed every day except Sunday. By 1899, it has been renamed the *Palm Beach Daily News* and is the only daily paper between St. Augustine and Key West.

1905 - Dean sells his interest to Palm Beach founding father Henry M. Flagler, who distances himself from the *Daily News* by bringing in Englishman Richard Overend Davies as publisher. The newspaper's high-quality paper stock soon gives it the nickname it enjoys today – "The Shiny Sheet."

1906 - Davies debuts *Palm Beach Life,* a magazine still in publication today.

1913 - Davies moves his publishing company's operations plant from West Palm Beach to a small building in Palm Beach. In 1925, the Davies family will construct a more substantial building on the same site at the corner of County Road and Brazilian Avenue.

continued on next page

Founded in 1906, *Palm Beach Life* magazine has always celebrated the people who make life in Palm Beach so captivating. These issues date from 1908, 1934 and 2013.

www.palmbeachdailynews.com.

Palm Beach Daily News Timeline

1920 - Davies buys out the Flagler heirs' interest in the *Daily News.*

1925 - Davies' son Oscar succeeds his father as publisher.

1929 - Oscar Davies helps spearhead fundraising for and construction of the Addison Mizner-designed Memorial Fountain and Park behind Town Hall; it is dedicated in 1930.

1935 - Oscar Davies retires as publisher but retains ownership; Ruby Edna Pierce, who in 1910 became business manager and editor of the *Daily News,* now leads the paper – a position she will hold until her retirement in 1954.

1948 - Attorney John H. Perry Sr., a Kentucky native with a home in Palm Beach, buys the *Daily News.* His Perry Publications includes newspapers from Jacksonville to Delray Beach, including *The Palm Beach Post* and *Palm Beach Times.*

1952 - Perry's son, John H. Perry Jr., inherits the papers upon his father's death and revolutionizes newspaper production with new technologies.

1969 - Cox Enterprises, a major national media company, buys the *Daily News.* Today, the newspaper is part of Atlanta-based Cox Media Group, an integrated broadcasting, publishing, direct-marketing and digital-media company that also publishes *The Palm Beach Post.*

1974 - The *Daily News* moves to 265 Royal Poinciana Way, where it will remain for 36 years.

1976 - Agnes Ash becomes publisher of the *Daily News* and expands the newspaper's scope, including regular coverage of the Town Council.

1991 - Joyce Reingold succeeds Ash as publisher. Under her guidance, the *Daily News* launches its website – PalmBeachDailyNews.com – in 1996 and later adds products for smartphones and other digital platforms. She also oversees the newspaper's 2011 move to offices at 400 Royal Palm Way.

1993 - The *Daily News* establishes a holiday toy drive to benefit children and teenagers in need, a tradition that continues today with the participation of the town's fire-rescue stations and Town of Palm Beach United Way.

1997 - The *Daily News* publishes as special edition to mark its 100th birthday.

2011 - To celebrate the centennial of the town's incorporation, the *Daily News* publishes a special supplement that includes an in-depth timeline of Palm Beach's history.

2014 - Upon Reingold's retirement, Tim Burke becomes publisher, the same position he holds at *The Palm Beach Post.* The *Daily News'* mission remains the same as Bobo Dean's in 1897: to report town news in as complete, objective, accurate and interesting a manner as possible, and to address issues important to readers.

The Palm Beach Police Foundation, Inc.

The Palm Beach Police Foundation is a charitable organization established in 2006 to benefit sworn officers and civilian employees of the Palm Beach Police Department. The 15-member board, comprised of civic leaders, town residents, members of the business and professional community, provides leadership and financial support to the men and women in blue.

The funds raised from the Annual Policemen's Ball, one of the island's most popular galas, go directly to the Foundation, which supports programs that include academic scholarships and grants to qualified children of Police Department employees.

In addition to the basic scholarships, The Charles R. Evans Scholarship, based on academic achievement, is awarded to students with a 3.0 or higher grade point average. The William I. Koch Scholarship provides partial funding for post-baccalaureate education combined with superior academic achievement.

Color Guard at 2014 Policemen's Ball at Mar-a-Lago

The Foundation also provides funding for new equipment and assistance to officers in need in times of distress, as well as to various crime watch programs including Palm Beach Crime Watch, which has promoted citizen participation in crime prevention for more than three decades. www.pbpf.us

Thomas C. Quick, 2011 Palm Tree Award Recipient, Llwyd Ecclestone, 2014 Palm Tree Award Recipient; Tim Moran, Vice President and Co-founder of PB Police Foundation; John F. Scarpa, President and Co-founder of PB Police Foundation and Kirk Blouin, Palm Beach Public Safety Director

Top Row: Stephen A. Levin, Mark E. Freitas, Jeff Greene, John W.S. Preston, Matthew K. Smith, Joel H. Kassewitz
Bottom Row: Michele Kessler, David S. Mack, John F. Scarpa, Tim Moran, Gerald Frank
Not Pictured: Michael Belisle, Annie Falk, Lawrence Herbert, William I. Koch

The Palm Beach Fellowship of Christians & Jews

The Palm Beach Fellowship of Christians and Jews was founded in 1993 as a grassroots effort by a handful of caring Christians and Jews in the Town of Palm Beach, seeking to promote fellowship, understanding and respect among all religions and cultures through education, dialogue and interaction and to address issues rooted in intolerance, anti-Semitism and unjust discrimination. A membership-based non-profit 501c 3, our member live both in the Town of Palm Beach and off the island. We also welcome non-members and guests. Independent of any national or regional organization, we have the support of six houses of worship in Palm Beach.

Laurel Baker and Dick Kleid

Leslie and Ronald Schram

Susan Keenan and Bill Meyer

John C. (Skip) and Leslie Randolph

Hon. Lesly Smith and Maggie Zeidman

We are known for our educational outreach programs such as the Interfaith Dialogue Series and an annual essay contest for high school and middle-school students; providing educators scholarships to study at the Holocaust-based Facing History and Ourselves summer seminars; community programs such as our Fellowship Friday volunteer event and our Fellowship Fun Day for families; bringing well-known speakers such as James Carroll, Amy-Jill Levine, Susannah Heschel, Rabbi Marc Gellman and Barbara Brown Taylor, to our annual dinner and luncheon and for numerous social receptions. We pride ourselves in building bridges as people of different faiths and beliefs develop a better understanding and new appreciation of one another. www.palmbeachfellowship.net

Fellowship Friday Volunteers

Fellowship Funday

Interfaith Dialogue Series with Rabbi Howard Shapiro and Tom O'Brien

Temple Emanu-El

First Temple building, 1974.

Temple Emanu-El was the first Jewish house of worship to be chartered and built on the Island of Palm Beach. The charter was granted January 24, 1963. For a number of years a small group of Jews met in a storefront on Sunrise Avenue. The Congregation grew in size, raised funds, acquired land on North County Road and dedicated the first building in 1974. The classic structure stands at 190 North County Road. The facade has two curved staircases leading up to the entrance doors. Tall graceful arches frame a series of stained glass windows. This structure housed the Sanctuary and offices for many years and remains part of the east side of the Melvin J. and Claire M. Levine Campus.

The original congregation continued to grow, and expansions became necessary several times in our history. Six major renovations took place. The most dramatic change was the addition of the Jack and Pearl Resnick Sanctuary, much enlarged and containing priceless stained glass windows, mosaics, Bimah art and tapestries designed by world class artists. In this exquisite setting, services take place.

In recent years our Rothman Religious School has grown, as have the exceptional programs for teens, post B'nai Mitzvah and High School students. The Heilweil Youth Lounge is where our young people meet, socialize and study. The Levin Hall, updated and renovated to expose the beautiful stained glass windows is used for celebrations, luncheons, dinners as well as lectures and film series. The Dan and Ewa Abraham Garden is a new expansion of our campus and houses a Pergola, the Sandi and Marvin Rosen Sukkah as well as Herb's Garden dedicated by Beverly Myers and family. The Ruth and Bert Mack Meditation Garden continues to provide a tranquil setting for quiet study, personal reflection and small group discussions.

We embrace our future with modern technology yet maintain our Jewish tradition in the magnificent surroundings provided by Temple Emanu-El of Palm Beach. www.tepb.org

PALM BEACH Society

PRESENTING SOCIETY 58TH YEAR

APRIL 15 - MAY 12, 2011

Centennial Celebration

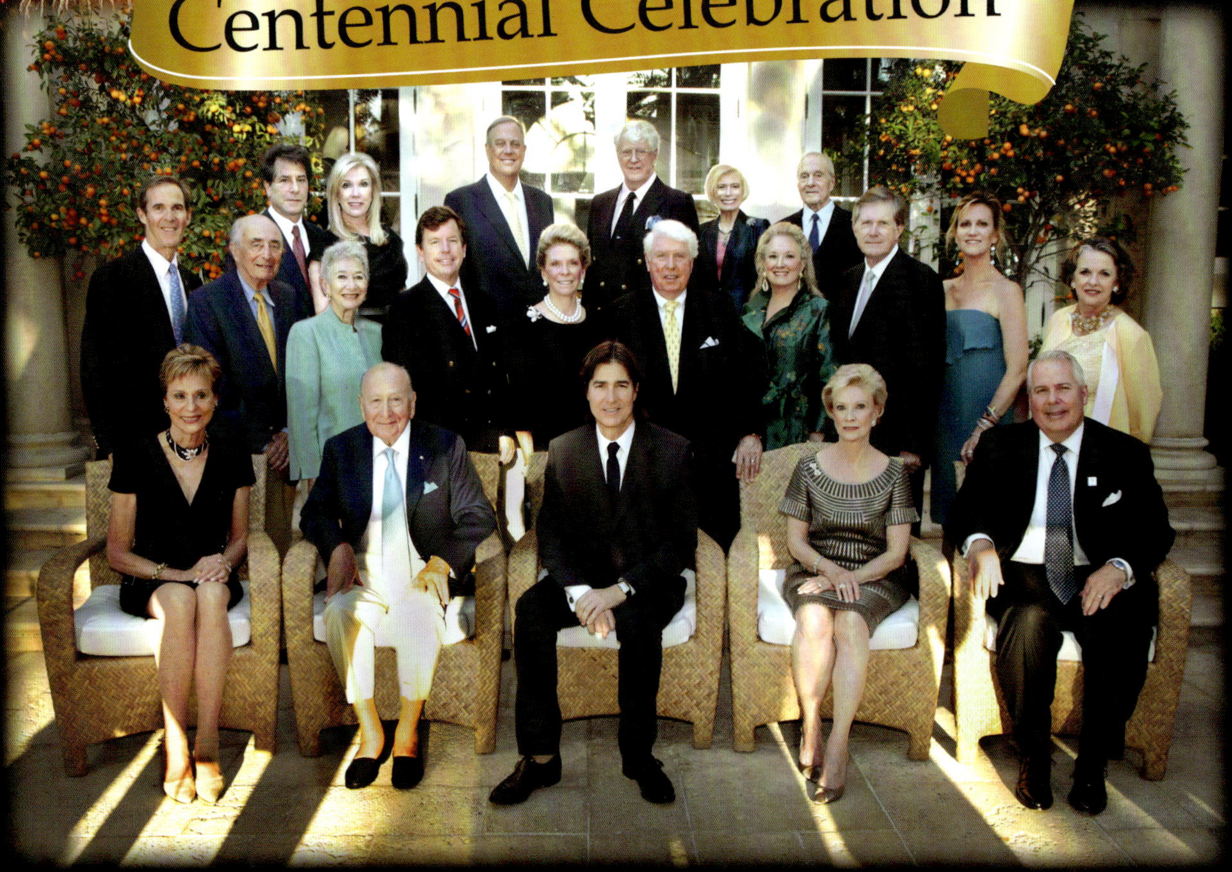

CENTENNIAL WEEKEND EVENT CHAIRS & BOARD OF DIRECTORS

Top Row: Howard & Michelle Kessler, David Koch, Bill Koch, Bobbi and Harry Horwich M.D.; Middle Row: Bill Metzger-Director, Alec & Miriam Flamm, Tom Quick, Peggy & Dudley Moore, Kathryn & Leo Vecellio, Talbott Maxey, Laurel Baker-Director; Front Row: Cynthia Friedman-Secretary, Edward Elson-Vice Chair, Bill Bone-Chairman, Betsy Matthews-Vice Chair, Kevin A. Johnson-Treasurer

THE PALM BEACH CENTENNIAL COMMISSION

invites

All residents to the "All Town Celebration"

Sunday, April 17th 2011

FLAGLER MUSEUM

The Palm Beach ambiance and way of life is unique to the world. In addition to the elegant, affluent lifestyle of its residents, Palm Beach has a vibrant, exciting social scene. At the heart of this scene are the myriad philanthropic fundraising events, which are hosted year-round and sustained by the earnest generosity of the island's residents.

Like its namesake, Palm Beach Society is similarly unique. Regarded as the island's premier "society" magazine, it covers all of these charitable and non-profit philanthropic events. Founded in 1983 by the late James Jennings Sheeran, Palm Beach Society has maintained an enthusiastic and devoted readership. Using a refined photojournalistic approach, each issue features comprehensive photo spreads of recent philanthropic fundraisers which Palm Beachers always look forward to seeing.

In addition to covering philanthropy, Palm Beach Society keeps readers up-to-date about forthcoming social events. It also publishes a handful of popular feature columns, such as Worth Asking, Fashion Avenue, A Conversation With, Manhattan, Dining and Divining, Travel and Social Highs.

For many years, Palm Beach has been synonymous with style and sophistication, and a commitment to philanthropy and charity. It is because of this powerful combination that Palm Beach Society has continued to attract so many people throughout the years on Florida's Gold Coast. www.pbsociety.com

~ VITA CELEBRATIO EST ~

2012

2013

2014

Peggy Adams Animal Rescue League Humane Society of the Palm Beaches

In 1924, a group of eight prominent ladies met on the porch of the home of Amy Lyman Phillips in Palm Beach, to decide what to do about the ongoing problem of animals left behind by winter visitors returning north. From that informal meeting emerged a league of concerned and dedicated people helping animals.

Our beginnings were humble. By 1925, we were incorporated. Makeshift cages were orange crates, and pens were fashioned from chicken wire at the abandoned TB hospital on the grounds of what is now Palm Beach International Airport. The hurricane of 1928 flattened this modest shelter, but donated funds and volunteer labor helped rebuild it.

With the onset of World War II, the city wanted to expand the airfield. Rather than condemn our property, they traded us a larger parcel at 24th and North Tamarind in West Palm Beach.

The new shelter had a small building with two large runs for male and female dogs,and a communal cat room. The generosity of two individuals allowed for the construction of a building for cats and a cottage. Bits at a time, several other donors stepped forward, affording us a modern kennel building, an annex with large covered runs, a new holding wing and a building for a meeting room.

As our work continued to expand, we gave up our meeting room when John D. MacArthur gave us money to convert it to a medical clinic, with accommodations for a veterinarian on the second floor. In August 1973, we started a spay-neuter clinic for the shelter's own animals, and by December of that year these services were expanded to provide low-cost services to owned animals in the community. To date, over 150,000 animals have been sterilized.

With each expansion, more funds were needed for operational expenses. We had yearly tag days, annual letters of appeal fund drives, and bake sales. But even with our best efforts, it was a continual struggle. We had occasional rummage sales, so it was a logical progression when we opened a Thrift Store at 1905 South Dixie Highway in 1973. Volunteers were plentiful, and we used our cars to pick up merchandise whenever possible. Little by little, we were able to add to our support.

For most of our 80 years we have been so busy taking care of animals, we have not publicized our efforts, but the word has been spread by our deeds. Jessie Stewart, as a tribute to then Executive Director, George Hulme, left us a bequest that enabled us to purchase our property on Military Trail. Catherine MacArthur provided the funds to construct our unique double-domed shelter. In 1989, Charles Norton Adams made a generous financial contribution to start our endowment fund in memory of his beloved wife, Peggy Adams, in return for a change in our name to Peggy Adams Animal Rescue League, from Animal Rescue League.

Today, this long standing organization offers dozens of services to support our life-saving mission. Because our community's generosity continues to grow, we completed construction of our state-of-the-art clinic and adoption center the Jane and Robert Grace Pavilion located at 3100 N. Military Trail. The clinic will help us to provide high-volume spay and neuter services to address the pet overpopulation problem in Palm Beach County and help fulfill our ultimate goal that every adoptable animal will have a chance at a life-long loving home.

Jane Grace

Our Vision & Mission...

Our Vision is to create a community where 100% of the adoptable animals find loving homes and no animals will be euthanized because of pet overpopulation. The Mission of the Peggy Adams Animal Rescue League of the Palm Beaches, Incorporated, is to provide shelter to lost, homeless and unwanted animals, to provide spay and neuter and other medical services for companion animals, and to care for, protect, and find quality homes for homeless and neglected companion animals, to advocate animal welfare, community involvement and education to further the bond between people and animals.

3100/3200 North Military Trail
West Palm Beach, FL 33409
PeggyAdams.org

Chairman Lesly Smith

Services include... Dog and Cat Adoptions, Affordable Spay-Neuter Services and Vaccine Clinic, Feral/Community Cat TNVR Program, Lost and Found, Dog Training, Fido's Food Bank, Memorial Gardens and Columbarium, End-of-life Services, Pet Boutique, Thrift Store, PetMobile Outreach Program

Palm Beach County History of The Salvation Army

The Salvation Army was founded in London's East End in 1865 by one-time Methodist Reform Church minister William Booth and his wife Catherine. Originally, Booth named the organization the East London Christian Mission. The name The Salvation Army developed from an incident during 19 and 20 May. William Booth was dictating a letter to his secretary George Scott Railtonand said, "We are a volunteer army." Bramwell Booth heard his father and said, "Volunteer! I'm no volunteer, I'm a regular!" Railton was instructed to cross out the word "volunteer" and substitute the word "salvation."

In 1921, the Kiwanis Club invited The Salvation Army to start operations in Palm Beach County. Between the years of 1928 and 2000, The Salvation Army of Palm Beach County grew both in facilities as well as services offered throughout the area. Thanks in part to the generosity and support of the Palm Beach Gala held each year. Today, The Salvation Army continues to work where the need is the greatest, guided by its faith in God and love for all people. www.salvationarmypalmbeachcounty.org

Serving Palm Beach since 1922

The Salvation Army would like to remember and honor those who have chaired our annual fundraiser over the years; who gave tirelessly of their efforts and support. Without them this benefit would not have continued its tradition for nearly 50 years.

The Salvation Army Annual Christmas Gala Event Chairs

1973-1982	Mrs. Eugenie Marron
1983	Mrs. Cathleen McFarlane
1984	Mrs. Frances Kennedy Staley
1985	Mrs. Kay Thoresen
1986	Mrs. Beverly White
1987	Barroness Monica VonHabsburg and Mr. & Mrs. Norris McFarlane
1988	Mr. and Mrs. James Partington
1989	Mr. and Mrs. Robert Hurbaugh
1990	Comm. and Mrs. James Nemec
1991	Dr. and Mrs. Arthur Turner
1992	Mrs. Mosse Hvide
1993	Mrs. Kathryn C. Vecellio
1994	Mayor Nancy Graham
1995-1996	Mrs. Arlette Gordon
1997	Mr. and Mrs. James Partington
1998	Mrs. Cathleen McFarlane and Mr. Reid Moore
1999	Mrs. Etonella Christlieb
2000	Mrs. Yvelyne deMarcellus Marix
2001-2004	Mrs. Nancy Sexauer Walsh
2005	Mr. and Mrs. Evangelos Kanaris
2007	Mrs. Marie Hope Davis
2008	Mrs. Marie Hope Davis, Co- Chairwoman Mrs. Ruby Rinker and Mrs. Eileen Cornacchia
2009	Honored Lawrence J. DeGeorge Honorary Chairs-Mrs.Florence DeGeorge and Mrs. Ruby Rinker
2010	Honored Mrs.Cathleen McFarlane-Ross with Honorary Chair- Mrs.Elizabeth Bowden
2011	Mayor Rudy Guiliani
2012	Mrs. Ruby Rinker, Mrs. Beverly White Yeager, Ms. Herme de Wyman Miro, Mrs. Kristina Anderson McPherson
2014	Mr.Henry "Budge" Jamison, Mrs. Candy Jamison, Dr. Shirley Stickle and Dr. Robert Stickle Ms. Jan McArt, Mrs. Jennie Baker-Finch

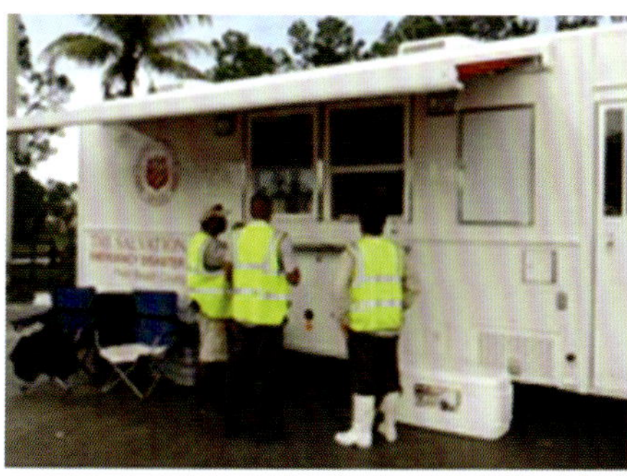

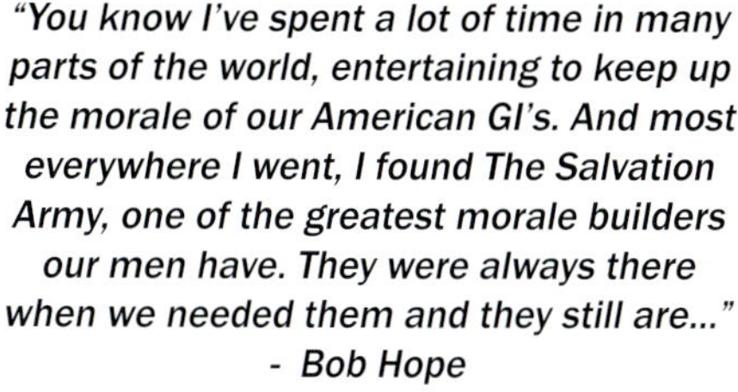

"You know I've spent a lot of time in many parts of the world, entertaining to keep up the morale of our American GI's. And most everywhere I went, I found The Salvation Army, one of the greatest morale builders our men have. They were always there when we needed them and they still are..."
- Bob Hope

"Well The Salvation Army means something to me, I served as Christmas Chair and they helped me when I wasn't as wealthy as I am now. I was a kid living in the projects, ...there was a Salvation Army building, and poor kids like me could come in read books, learn to box, they could play baseball, they could play basketball, all sorts of recreation... " Bill Cosby

Schepens Eye Research Institute

Schepens Eye Research Institute, now an affiliate of Massachusetts Eye and Ear and Harvard Medical School, has been a source of visionary inspiration for Palm Beachers since the 1960s.

Founded in 1950 by Dr. Charles L. Schepens (pronounced Skay' pens), the Institute that bears his name was renowned for major breakthroughs in treatment of retinal disease, optic nerve regeneration, new treatments for macular degeneration, diabetic retinopathy, glaucoma, other types of retinal and optic nerve degenerations and damage, dry eye and eye tissue transplants. The Institute has pioneered some of the most acclaimed research which has led to the development of products and technology to prevent, cure and eradicate blindness.

Because of its defining research, Schepens Eye Research Institute has attracted the interest of thousands of supporters over the years and garnered the interest of many captains of industry, philanthropists and celebrities, including Ella Fitzgerald, Lauren Bacall, Jason Robards, Eli Wallach, Julie Harris, Olivia Newton-John, Mike Douglas, Jane Seymour, Della Reese, Ed Asner, Loni Anderson, Nancy Kerrigan, Angela Landsbury and Jon Voight, as well as statemen from all over the globe.

"The Institute has had tremendous support from private philanthropy since it started," noted John Fernandez, President and Chief Executive Officer of Mass Eye and Ear, "but nowhere as steadfast and as generous as in Palm Beach. We are incredibly grateful to supporters and trustees -- like Kathryn Vecellio, Herme de Wyman Miro, Judith Grubman and many others, who have kept the Institute front and center in Palm Beach and people's minds for many years."According to Fernandez, "Our Palm Beach supporters are extremely rare. They have opened their homes, their motor yachts and hosted events for Schepens in Palm Beach and in Boston since the 1970s. Kathryn Vecellio, for example, has been a trustee for over 20 years and has served as chairman, junior chairman or honorary chairman for almost every Schepens' fundraising event in Palm Beach. She is considered to be the glue that keeps us together. She has introduced her friends to the Institute's mission and invited them to attend Schepens' fundraising events in Palm Beach, New York and Boston. We are truly grateful to her commitment, leadership, generosity, guidance and fundraising skills."

Dr. Charles L. Schepens

Considered the Father of Modern Retinal Surgery, Dr. Schepens invented the indirect binocular ophthalmoscope, whose modern-day version is still used by ophthalmologists around the world to examine patients' retinas during routine eye examinations. His prototype is on display in the Smithsonian Institute.

In Palm Beach, supporters have raised funds at formal galas and luncheons as well as at receptions in private homes, hotels, Worth Avenue boutiques and art galleries to provide a platform to raise funds for research and the annual Eye and Vision Research Symposia which is presented as a gift to the community.

Every year since the late 1960s, scientists from SERI have been invited to present their research at the symposia series, which has been held at all the major Palm Beach hotels, including The Breakers, The Ritz-Carlton, the Brazilian Court and The Colony Hotel, as well as the Mar-A-Lago Club. The annual luncheon, which has featured fashions from Neiman Marcus Palm Beach, was considered the kickoff to the Palm Beach social season.

In addition to Mr. and Mrs. Leo Vecellio, Jr., Mrs. Miro and Mrs. Grubman, supporters have included: Mossette and Dr. Henri Kayzer-Andre, Bessie and Raymond Kravis, Joan and Murray Goodman, Helen Boehm, Olivia and Walter Kiebach, Florence and Bunky Knudsen, Brownie McLean, Frank Randolph, Fran Todman, Gertrud Turklitz, Kay and Peter Lyons, Nancy Shaw Raquet, Sandra Krakoff, Monika and John Preston, Julie and Howard Rudolph, Michele and Howard Kessler, Anne Moran, Colleen Bain, Caroline and Bob Collings, Linda and Edward Dweck, Laurie Silvers and Mitchell Rubenstein, Joan and Ben Rubin, Mary and Mark Freitas, Arlette Gordon, Vicki and Chris Kellogg, Sharon and Alton O'Neil, Evelyn and Leo Vecellio, Sr., and Babbette and William Wolff, Cheryl Gowdy, Curt and Jerre Gowdy, Beverly and Herbert Myers, Emily DiMaggio, Beth Pine and Anka Palitz.

For more information on Mass. Eye and Ear, please visit www.masseyeandear.org

Celebrating 60 Years

Photos from events held at The Breakers Hotel and on the M/Y Lady Kathryn V.

Michele and Howard Kessler

Julie and Howard Rudolph with Dr.Angela Vecellio

Leo and Kathryn Vecellio

Herme deWyman Miro and Dr. Joan Miller

Kathryn Vecellio, Kay Lyons, Connor Boss and Julie Rudolph

Linda Salandra-Dweck and Monika Preston

Vicky Kellogg, Chris Kellogg and Anka Palitz

Cheryl Gowdy with Kay and Peter Lyons

Schepens Luncheon Committee

Luncheon Chairs on Deck - Colleen Bain, Laurie Silvers, Nancy Shaw Raquet, Monika Preston, Herme deWyman Miro, Anne Moran, Michele Millard, Kay Lyons and Andrea Stark

Town of Palm Beach United Way

Since 1945, the Town of Palm Beach United Way has invested more than $60 million into Palm Beach County because of generous donors who live or work on the island of Palm Beach. We advance the common good, creating opportunities for a better life for all by focusing on the three building blocks of a good life - education, health and income. The Town of Palm Beach United Way recruits people and organizations that bring the passion, expertise and resources needed to get things done.

The Town of Palm Beach United Way began in 1945 as the Palm Beach Community Chest. A group of community leaders wanted to raise funds for the needy in our area. The first year the Community Chest raised $70,500 and today raises over $4.7 million.

Through the years the Chest evolved and grew. In 2005, the Palm Beach Community Chest became the Town of Palm Beach United Way. Today our mission remains the same as in 1945 – to help people community wide improve their quality of life.

44 Cocoanut Row, M201, Palm Beach , FL 33480
www.palmbeachunitedway.org

Project Team

Team Leadership

Olympia Devine and her son, Troy Devine:
Team Leaders, Palm Beach Tribute

Troy Devine (1980-2013) was the founder and art director for this book project. He was a recognized innovator, an accomplished business leader, photographer and published author.

Olympia and Troy have been part of Palm Beach for more than twenty-five years. Troy attended the Palm Beach Day Academy. They were the official producers and public relations firm for the Palm Beach Centennial, helping it become one of the largest events the town has ever seen. This event gave birth to the need for an historical coffee table book – one which would highlight the unique families and organizations who have made a difference. They are recognized for their philanthropy and expertise in new business development for more than 30 years - with more than 3,000 projects produced in Palm Beach County. Their creativity includes: photographic and editorial publications, product manufacture and development; commercial and fashion photography and brand management.

Olympia Devine continues her son's spirit of innovation as art director of this community tribute - and more especially his passion for community and... the Town of Palm Beach.

Laurel Baker: *Senior Editor, Palm Beach Tribute,*
and Executive Director, Palm Beach Chamber of Commerce

Laurel Baker serves as the Palm Beach Community Project Senior Editor. She is a published writer, talented editor and recognized Palm Beach community advisor.

Laurel came to Palm Beach County in the mid-70s and the serendipity of life presented countless new challenges for her - from social work and inner-city teaching in the 60s to liberating experiences at two wonderful art museums. In between banking, a nature preserve and an introduction to the world of nonprofits through a private foundation, laid the foundation for the next career adventure at the Palm Beach Chamber of Commerce. She is now the Executive Director (and force) behind the Palm Beach Chamber of Commerce, helping it grow to become one of the largest organizations... in the Town of Palm Beach.

Having raised her daughters in Palm Beach and volunteered with the Preservation Foundation's school program, Laurel served as a member of the Architectural Commission and Landmarks. Laurel has a strong sense of what community is all about and strives to bring people and talents together to raise awareness and quality of place.

Photographers

Mort Kaye
(1916-2013)
Lucien Capehart and Robert Davidoff began their Palm Beach careers under Mort Kaye's tutelage. Known throughout town as 'the portrait photographer', Mort was able to capture the essence of the individual's personality and character with patience and humor. With camera in hand, he visited numerous social events throughout the season, marking historic events and notables. An indefatigable worker, Mort was well into his 90s when he formally 'retired' from the profession he loved, passing on his great legacy to his son Corby.

Lucien Capehart
(1946-2012)
Lucien Capehart arrived in Palm Beach almost four decades ago. He came to the beautiful island resort community on what was supposed to be a diving and photography vacation, yet fell in love with what he saw and experienced and never left. Today, the name Lucien Capehart is synonymous with excellence in artistic photography and design. He was perhaps the most sought after artist to create the perfect portrait, capture the special moments of the most elaborate weddings, galas, celebrity events, and much more before his untimely death in February, 2012. Today, his photographic team continues his amazing legacy at Lucien Capehart Photography. Lucien was excited to be part of the Palm Beach Tribute team and he cherished his time shared with the Palm Beach community - he is greatly missed by all!

Robert Davidoff
(1926-2004)
Bob Davidoff began his island career in 1955 and went on to bring smiles to countless residents, visitors and celebrities. Best known for his long- standing relationship with the Kennedy family, Bob recorded the life stories of other Palm Beach citizens like the Azqueta and Fanjul families. From rock stars, to royalty and the silver screen, Davidoff Studios captured an extraordinary time in Palm Beach's history. Stars of the silver screen included Jack Benny, Bing Crosby, Robin Williams and many more kept the magic of the movies alive in paradise. Dukes and duchesses appeared, along with Prince Charles and Lady Diana, Princess Yasmin Aga Kan, Prince Andrew and heads of state such as Presidents George H. W. Bush, Gerald Ford and Ronald Reagan. Today, Bob's son and wife, Daryl and Babe, continue The Davidoff Studio tradition.

The Palm Beach Foundation, Inc.

Mission

This project is being coordinated together with The Palm Beach Foundation 501(c)3 whose mission is to further the arts, culture and history for children. A portion of proceeds from book sales will benefit and develop necessary community programs.

The Palm Beach Foundation believes that: artistic and cultural activities are an essential component of healthy, strong and vibrant communities; the arts provide us with meaning and a sense of community; the arts help us experience and interpret the rapidly changing world; the arts give voice to diverse and under-represented communities; the arts help promote cross-cultural understanding; the arts encourage participation in civic and community life.

Olympia Devine, *Founder*

Palm Beach - a Community Tribute

Publication produced by: Devine Public Relations
www.devinepublicrelations.com

Art Directors: Troy A. Devine and Olympia Devine

Senior Editor: Laurel Baker
Editorial and Photographic Content:
Project Team page 240-241
Special Acknowledgements: page 9

Graphic Designer: Zach Seltzer
Graphic Design: Lauren Ellis
Cover Concept: Jonathan Stein
"Postcards from Palm Beach - a true paradise"
www.gallerybiba.com
All Chrome Everything, Inc.

For more information:
The Palm Beach Foundation
205 Worth Avenue, Suite 201, Palm Beach, FL 33480 USA
www.ThePalmBeachFoundation.org • 561-653-1600

TEA GARDEN AT THE BREAKERS, PALM BEACH, FLORIDA
Bathing Scene, Palm Beach, Fla.